Defying Gravity was written to encourage p___ day of intense pressure. Daniel Henderson ___ ___ ___ ___ ___ ___ in bringing solid truth to remind us that God's Word is still the best navigation system in the midst of stormy times.

JIM CYMBALA

Senior Pastor, The Brooklyn Tabernacle

As a pilot, I've learned to rely on the instruments. As a pastor, I've learned to trust the things I know to be true. As a leader, you will want to embrace the proven wisdom and encouragement of this book—written by my valued friend and colleague, Daniel Henderson.

JONATHAN FALWELL

Senior Pastor, Thomas Road Baptist Church

They lead by example, serve with humility, guide with wisdom, and offer the love of Christ. But many remain lonely, fear trusting others, and live under a weight of criticism. That's the portrait of today's pastor. If you're a leader in ministry you know costs. Daniel Henderson, with a holy passion for helping ministry leaders, provides a valuable resource for "standing in the gap" for one another.

DR. TIM CLINTON

President, American Association of Christian Counselors

In a day when church leaders are falling out of ministry at an alarming rate, God has gifted us with spiritual leaders like Daniel Henderson who have a proven ministry track record, a heart for pastors, and a passion for Christ to help inspire leaders to survive the storms of ministry. *Defying Gravity* is a gift I plan to give every young pastor I mentor and include as required reading for each church planter we train.

BRIAN BLOYE

Lead Pastor, West Ridge Church and

President, Engage Atlanta

Defying Gravity

How to Survive the Storms
of Pastoral Ministry

DANIEL
HENDERSON

MOODY PUBLISHERS
CHICAGO

All Scripture quotations, unless otherwise indicated, are taken from the *New King James Version*. Copyright © 1982 by Thomas Nelson, Inc. Used by permission. All rights reserved.

Scripture quotations marked NASB are taken from the *New American Standard Bible®*, Copyright © 1960, 1962, 1963, 1968, 1971, 1972, 1973, 1975, 1977, 1995 by The Lockman Foundation. Used by permission. (www.Lockman.org)

Scripture quotations marked NLT are taken from the *Holy Bible, New Living Translation*, copyright © 1996. Used by permission of Tyndale House Publishers, Inc., Wheaton, Illinois 60189, U.S.A. All rights reserved.

Scripture quotations marked NIV are taken from the *Holy Bible, New International Version®*. NIV®. Copyright © 1973, 1978, 1984 by International Bible Society. Used by permission of Zondervan. All rights reserved.

Scripture quotations marked AMP are taken from *The Amplified Bible*. Copyright © 1965, 1987 by The Zondervan Corporation. The Amplified New Testament copyright © 1958, 1987 by The Lockman Foundation. Used by permission.

Scripture quotations marked *The Message* are from *The Message*, copyright © by Eugene H. Peterson 1993, 1994, 1995. Used by permission of NavPress Publishing Group.

A study guide for personal or group application is available at www.strategicrenewal.com/defying gravity.

Editor: Jim Vincent
Interior Design: Ragont Design
Cover Design: John Hamilton Design
Cover and Interior Image: iStock

Library of Congress Cataloging-in-Publication Data

Henderson, Daniel.
    Defying gravity : how to survive the storms of pastoral ministry / by Daniel Henderson.
        p. cm.
    Includes bibliographical references (p.   ).
    ISBN 978-0-8024-0952-2
    1. Pastoral theology. 2. Christian leadership. I. Title.
BV4011.3.H46 2010
253—dc22

                                        2009026292

We hope you enjoy this book from Moody Publishers. Our goal is to provide high-quality, thought-provoking books and products that connect truth to your real needs and challenges. For more information on other books and products written and produced from a biblical perspective, go to www.moodypublishers.com or write to:

Moody Publishers
820 N. LaSalle Boulevard
Chicago, IL 60610

1 3 5 7 9 10 8 6 4 2

Printed in the United States of America

To Rosemary,
my partner in life, marriage, and ministry
for almost thirty years.
Your support has been a powerful force
in helping me to "defy gravity."

And to Rosemary's father, Dr. Fred V. Brewer,
whose faithful pastoral leadership for more than
sixty-five years has inspired thousands to
deeper faith and spiritual endurance.

Contents

Part 1: Avoiding Leadership Vertigo

Part 2: Viewing the Leadership Instrument Panel

Part 3: Reaching the Destination

Acknowledgments

I remember sitting in a chapel service as a college student, listening to a motivational message by Charles "Tremendous" Jones. He made a statement that so challenged me I bought the cassette tape (remember those?) and replayed it until I had written the quote down word-for-word. His valuable insight stated: "All the truth in the world will do you little good until God brings a person across your path and you are able to see that truth in action. Suddenly, that truth becomes a driving force in your life."

Personally, I am deeply indebted to many of my mentors and colleagues who have been "truth in action" over these decades of pastoral ministry. I am especially grateful to those who sacrificed their time and effort to become the "truth in action" factor for this book. Each has added practical insight and "color" to these chapters. Their example, candor and practical advice make this book unique. I offer my heartfelt thanks to:

- Doug Boquist, lead pastor of Bedford Church of the Nazarene, Bedford, Ohio
- Vernon Brewer, founder and president of World Help, Forest, Virginia
- Luis Bush, international facilitator of Transform World, Lynchburg, Virginia

- Galen Call, senior pastor (retired) of Venture Christian Church, Los Gatos, California
- Karen Covell, director of Hollywood Prayer Network, North Hollywood, California
- Jennifer Kennedy Dean, founder and president of The Praying Life Foundation, Blue Springs, Missouri
- Mark DeYmaz, lead pastor, Mosaic Church, Little Rock, Arkansas
- David Earley, professor and director of The Center for Church Planting, Liberty University, Lynchburg, Virginia
- Hans Finzel, President of World Venture, Littleton, Colorado
- David Frauenshuh, founder and chief executive officer of Frauenshuh, Inc., Bloomington, Minnesota
- Alan Ginn, missionary, Leadership Resources International, Sacramento, California
- David Gudgel, senior pastor of Bethany Bible Church, Phoenix, Arizona
- Dennis Henderson, senior pastor of Sherman Bible Church, Sherman, Texas
- Paul Hontz, senior pastor of Central Wesleyan Church, Holland, Michigan
- John MacArthur, pastor-teacher of Grace Community Church, Sun Valley, California
- Paul Molitor, baseball player (retired) in the Hall of Fame, Chanhassen, Minnesota
- David Peddie, president of Peddie Roofing & Waterproofing, Calgary, Alberta
- Paul Powers, senior pastor of Union Baptist Church, St. Johnsbury, Vermont
- Jim Shaddix, senior pastor of Riverside Baptist Church, Denver, Colorado
- Sid Verdoorn, president and board chairman (retired), C.H. Robinson Company, Eden Prairie, Minnesota
- Jeff Wells, senior pastor of Woodsedge Community Church, The Woodlands, Texas

Thanks to Byron Paulus and the leadership team at Life Action Ministries for connecting me with Moody Publishers. I am grateful for our mutual burden for church leaders and your gracious belief in the message I had to share.

Thanks to Justin Henderson, Leif Aronsen, Andrew Walton, Leonard Davidson, and Doug Carter for your input on the concepts and content of the book.

I am so grateful to Greg Thornton, Dave DeWit, Jim Vincent, Keith Wiederwax, Pam Pugh, and the other members of the Moody Publishing team who have been very helpful and encouraging in seeing this project to completion.

Of course, I thank Christ for my wife and children. Their support has been incredibly powerful as they have flown with me through the storms of pastoral ministry. Rosemary, you have helped me defy gravity so many times by believing in me and enduring the trials of leadership with such grace. Justin, Jordan, and Heather—I am so proud of you. God has been so kind to bless our home with three children who have grown up to love and serve Christ with deep passion, in spite of the twists and turns of church work. You are champions.

Finally, I thank those leaders who will pick up this book, read it, and incorporate it into the fabric of their lives and influence. As you "defy gravity" you will honor the name of our Lord Jesus Christ and elevate the high and holy calling He has placed upon us. I am encouraged by your commitment to endure the storms and soar in your leadership for His glory.

Foreword

If there were no opportunities we would need no leaders. If there were no problems we would need no leaders.

That's what leaders are for—opportunities and problems. Good leaders understand that there are plenty of both.

Growing up as a pastor's son I didn't pay much attention to the problems. My father led the same New Jersey church for thirty-three years—from before I was born until long after I had grown up and become a pastor myself. I liked being a pastor's son. I liked the church. I never thought of my father dealing with difficulties.

Then I became a pastor and was as surprised as a plane passenger flying through a first thunderstorm. As a solo leader in a smaller congregation I counseled couples with problems far bigger than my competence, anguished over finances inadequate to pay the mortgage or the pastor's salary, thrilled to the transformation of sinners into saints, and was crushed by criticisms from people I loved. I learned what it is like to be a leader in over his head.

Now I am the veteran pastor, having led the same congregation for thirty-three years. I have learned lessons I wish I knew when I first took off into pastoral ministry:

1. Pastoral leadership is hard. We are ministering to people in the realities of life. We are agents of God. There are no exceptions or exemptions—pastoral ministry is hard for us all.
2. God is faithful. He is on our side. He never abandons us. He is committed to our survival and success.
3. Mentors are gifts. My mentors have taught me what to do. They have encouraged and blessed me. That's what chapter 7 of *Defying Gravity* is all about—mentoring for all of us pastoral leaders.
4. Live Christianly. Every circumstance is an opportunity to faithfully serve God, but the storms may be the times when Jesus shines brightest in our lives and leadership. Living for Jesus when there is sickness, criticism, opposition, and financial stress is how we teach others to live for Jesus when they are sick, criticized, opposed, and broke.
5. It's worth it. We teach the truth of God week after week. We witness the Holy Spirit transforming broken lives into the image of Jesus Christ. We pray for our people. We are there when babies are born and when believers die. We have front row seats to the works of God in the Church of Jesus Christ.

During World War II aviators liked to say, "God is my copilot." Not so; God is our pilot. Daniel Henderson shows us how to defy gravity and fly high with our Lord at the controls.

Leith Anderson
Senior Pastor, Wooddale Church
Eden Prairie, Minnesota

The most difficult adjustment that you must make as you acquire flying skill is a willingness to believe that, under certain conditions, your senses can be wrong. . . . When your senses seem to disagree with the instruments, trust the instruments—they may save your life.

MEDICAL HANDBOOK FOR PILOTS

He who leans on, trusts in, and is confident of his own mind and heart is a [self-confident] fool, but he who walks in skillful and godly Wisdom shall be delivered.

PROVERBS 28:26 (AMP)

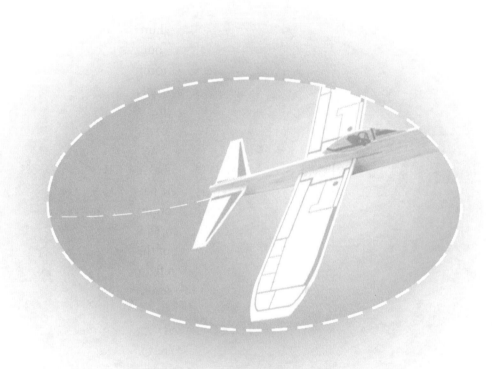

Introduction

The Leadership Flight

Our executive team of the large Southern California church sat around the table one June morning as we did most Tuesdays for our weekly meeting. John MacArthur, our pastor and leader, opened the morning edition of the *Los Angeles Times*. An article appeared just inside the front page with breaking news about a well-known West Coast megachurch.

John read us the heartbreaking story of a pastor who had served his congregation for almost three decades, leading the church to exponential growth, effective church planting, and profound global impact through a well-funded missions program. Two days earlier, the pastor had publicly confessed to an affair that dated back eight years. According to the story, the tryst lasted eleven months. His resignation was sudden, shocking, and newsworthy, even in the minds of the secular reporters of the *Times*. Perhaps their interest was sparked by this pastor's visibility in fighting gay rights in the state as a spokesman of the Moral Majority. The secular press often delights in contradictions of this sort.

A fascinating conversation ensued, as we grappled with many key questions. What would the church do? Would they try to restore him to leadership? How would they recover? Would the pastor's marriage survive? Of course, we prayed for the church, the pastor, and his family that day. We were heartbroken by another confession, another scandal, another trusting and growing flock with violated trust, an uncertain future, and a long road to recovery. This story was more fuel for a skeptical, watching world.

For me, it was a bit more personal. I knew the church well through some friends who served on the staff. Two months earlier I had visited the church with a colleague to learn more about their worship ministries and administrative structure. In many ways, this was a model church.

My disbelief and heartache that June morning would eventually turn to devastation and heart-wrenching pain in the ensuing years. This tragedy would become very personal—perhaps too personal—and more trying than I could have ever anticipated.

A Growing List of Leadership Disasters

Since that morning in 1988, I've heard hundreds of stories just like this one. The reports of leadership fallout seem more frequent, and in some cases more twisted and shocking than the previous. Pastors of churches large and small appear to be falling like flies. According to Focus on the Family, 1,500 pastors a month leave the ministry due to church conflict, marriage problems, moral disqualification, or unresolved personal problems.[1] This is a severe and ongoing tragedy, perpetually devastating the church.

We've also watched denominational leaders, famous Christian recording artists, and high-profile televangelists become embroiled in scandalous financial and sexual misconduct. Of course, leadership failure is not just epidemic in the church world. Whether it is the Oval Office, the governor's mansion, the Senate floor, or the House of Representatives, scandals abound throughout the American political scene. All too often we see powerful, intelligent people in a "crash and burn" mode due to private dealings that caused the unraveling of their credibility.

In the business arena we remember stories like Enron, the multifaceted energy company that went from claimed revenues of nearly $101 billion in 2000 to bankruptcy in 2001 because of institutionalized, systematic, and creatively planned fraud and corruption. Numerous companies have followed similar paths under the leadership of CEOs who compromised and brought the company down with them.

In sports and entertainment, we can recognize many smart, talented, motivated people who lost their moorings. The scandals surrounding Martha Stewart's insider trading, Michael Vick's illegal dogfighting, Mel Gibson's DUI conviction, and Winona Ryder's shoplifting conviction are all reminders that smart people do stupid things when their "internal processors" become flawed and confused.

Leaders Losing Altitude

As president of a national renewal organization, I visit and interact with hundreds of leaders each year, the vast majority of whom are faithful and skilled servants of God. Yet many of these leaders open up to me about their personal and private challenges. The pain is deep. The struggles are real. They are called to leadership, and want to remain faithful, but many are losing their way and hanging on for dear life.

One of my great desires is helping leaders who are "losing altitude." Our organization, Strategic Renewal, raises funds to help hurting church leaders get the help they need before they crash and burn. "An ounce of prevention," we might call it. This is an urgent and compelling need.

Leaders Taking Flight

I am a self-professing "leadership-aholic." I love leading. I love reading about leadership and studying other leaders. In this book, I liken the leadership assignment to a flight assignment; leaders and coleaders as pilots and copilots. The similarities are fascinating.

While I love to fly, I am not a pilot. I have controlled planes from the right seat numerous times, as friends have transported me to speaking engagements via small private aircraft. I enjoy "elite" status on multiple airlines because of the frequency of my commercial travel. My father, James Eagle Henderson, was an Air Force bomber pilot. I grew up hearing wonderful stories about military flight. I was recruited by the Air Force Academy but chose Bible college and seminary instead. So I am familiar with and enjoy studying flying. I have read books about planes and famous flights. And in the process of writing this book, I have conferred with various pilots and flight instructors.

The metaphor fits for most pastors and business leaders: Most of our lives are composed of numerous leadership flights. Some business executives may stay with the same company for decades; others have numerous shorter leadership assignments in various locations and settings. An experienced educator, civic leader, government official, or business manager may piece together an array of leadership flights that have made up a career.

For pastors, the average tenure in Protestant churches has declined to just four years, according to George Barna.[2] So most pastors will have numerous leadership flights in their ministry career. Some have fewer, longer flights. I followed one pastor in Sacramento, California, whose leadership flight in one church lasted forty years.

Some pastoral leaders are involved in several flights at once. My friend Leith Anderson has been the senior pastor of Wooddale Church in Eden Prairie, Minnesota, for more than thirty years. During a portion of that time, he also served as interim president of Denver Seminary, and a few years ago became president of the National Association of Evangelicals while continuing as senior pastor. Leith is a capable guy, "in flight" on numerous assignments at the same time.

Flight and Leadership

In brief, I see numerous parallels between flying and leading:

- *Training and Qualification.* Just as pilots must be trained, be equipped, and earn a license and certification, so leaders must be equipped and qualified to lead effectively. Formal education can be a part of this preparation, though not always. Mentoring, proven service, and faithful character are essential for the growing leader. We find these biblical specifics in 1 Timothy 3:1–8 and Titus 1, given for those who take on the primary leadership roles in the church. These traits are good qualifiers for Christian leaders in any realm of service.

- *Passion and Perseverance.* Most pilots learn to fly because of a passion for the skies. Experienced pilots have persevered, logging hours and increasing their certification in order to excel in the skills of flying larger and more sophisticated aircraft. Leaders also have a God-given desire for influencing other people and making a significant difference in the world. Great leaders remain faithful, develop their understanding of leadership principles, and maintain noble character and winning habits.

- *Risk and Reward.* At times flying can be risky. Although commercial flights are statistically the safest way to travel, we all know that the consequences of a mechanical failure or pilot error can be disastrous. Quite literally, lives hang in the balance. Yet the effectiveness and exhilaration of flight makes it worth it. For commercial pilots, helping people travel efficiently whether to conduct vital business, share holidays with family, or enjoy a much-needed vacation has to be fulfilling. Leadership is also risky. Decisions affect many people. And like pilots, pastors can affect the lives of those in their care. Setbacks, even failure, are possible. Yet, the thrill of leading people to the achievement of a great cause, especially one of eternal significance, is a joy beyond human expression.

- *Responsibility and Accountability.* Of course, experienced pilots carry a serious responsibility for human lives. The bigger the plane, the greater the volume of precious human cargo. As a result, pilots are accountable to strict standards of flight protocol, personal discipline, and compliance with regulations. Pastors are accountable also. Spiritual leaders influence people and, according to James 3:1, have a greater accountability for how they lead and what they teach. There are no solo flights in leadership.

- *Objectivity and Trust.* The best pilots learn to trust their instruments, the information from ground control, and the proven technology necessary for safe and trouble-free flight. Good leaders must also learn to trust objective indicators, including God's authoritative, holy Word, for their leadership flight. When self-trust and emotional justifications outweigh the proven realities for effective leadership, destructive behavior and disaster happen. Leaders lose altitude. People are at risk. Too often, a crash occurs and the human casualties are devastating.

Using the flight analogy, I've written this book to help pastors and other leaders maintain their leadership altitude in a world that wants to bring us down. I believe the biggest challenges to an effective and enduring leadership flight are our own flawed perceptions, subjective emotions, and misjudgments that can put us in real danger.

God wants us to soar and has provided an indispensable instrument panel for our success and endurance as leaders. It's time, with God's help and our commitment, to defy gravity.

Part 1
Avoiding Leadership Vertigo

Discouragement is a temporary loss of perspective.

ANONYMOUS

*But you be watchful in all things, endure afflictions,
do the work of an evangelist, fulfill your ministry.*

2 TIMOTHY 4:5

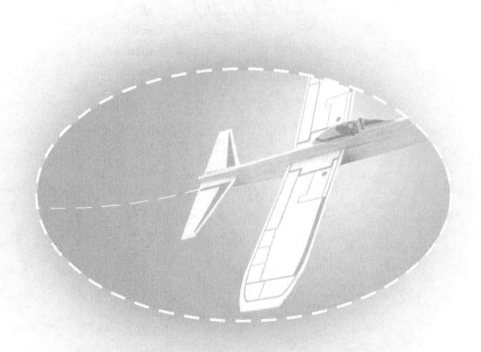

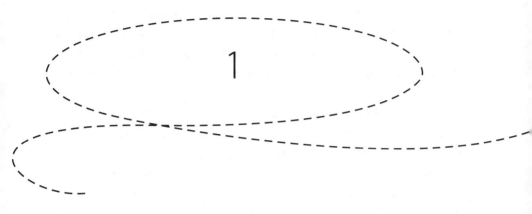

Unexpected
Leadership Storms

Several large, complex textbooks lay open on my desk as I write this chapter. Each is used to train pilots for private and commercial instrument flight. In the early chapters these texts always address human factors. First and foremost, the pilot must understand his personal vulnerability to disorientation and human error.

Next, these textbooks deal early and extensively with the challenges of unpredictable and dangerous weather. Pilots typically do well in clear and calm conditions. Unpredictable and unanticipated environmental conditions test a pilot's skill and knowledge. Dealing with these threats is foundational to becoming a pilot. Icing, thunderstorms, wind shear, lightning, fog, and many other dynamics threaten safe flight. Pilots are required to obtain weather reports, study the atmosphere, and fly with extreme awareness and caution. Still, bad weather happens, equipment fails, and communication gets confused. Danger lurks in the skies.

Leadership is tested in storms. You may be in the midst of one as you read this book. If not, you will be soon. Storms come with leadership. The names and circumstances are surely different for all of us, but the perplexity and pain are essentially the same. You may be a pastor in a hurting and dysfunctional church or an executive who's navigating an unprecedented downturn in the financial stability of the company. You might be serving as a community leader, trying to deal with unfriendly and needless opposition. Maybe you are trying to lead a family through a complex maze of conflict, hurt, and confusion.

Whatever the situation, leaders have to learn to navigate and survive the storms. I remember many years ago while still in college hearing a businessman say, "I pay people according to the problems they can solve and the pain they can endure." At the time, I knew the statement was profound but I had little understanding of how problems and pain were so germane to leadership. Now I understand the reality of this wisdom.

Just as pilots avoid storms by flying around them or even landing the plane beyond the thunderheads, leaders are wise to steer clear of threatening situations. But often raging storms are unavoidable. When a storm comes, leaders must know how to manage their own thoughts and emotions so they can make decisions in a way that those entrusted to their care are safe and growing toward the objectives God has established for their lives. Sadly, there are still those rare occasions when a leadership storm results in disaster for a leader, his family, and those he leads.

Holding the Black Box

In most media reports of plane crashes, we hear about the infamous "black box." Actually, this is a reference to two different instruments, normally located in the tail end of the plane. One is the cockpit voice recorder, and the other is the flight data recorder. These black boxes are essential in discovering the cause of an aviation accident, as well as providing plane manufacturers and government agencies vital information to help make air travel as safe as possible. Fireproof and impact proof, the boxes are built and located to survive a disaster, even when little else does.

I guess you could say that on two occasions I was left holding the "black box" after a leadership crash. In both cases, lessons would emerge about what went wrong and how to prevent similar disasters in the future.

I've had the privilege of stepping into three megachurch settings as the new senior pastor at high-risk moments. Each experience was marked by incredible stress. But all involved some wonderful people who have enriched my life in countless ways. Through these parishoners, their stories, and the journey God was taking us on, valuable lessons for avoiding a leadership crash emerged—the nine truths found in part 2 of this book.

You read about the first situation in the introduction. The church spotlighted in the *Los Angeles Times* that Tuesday morning eventually called me as their next senior pastor. This is the rest of the story: In addition to the tragedy of the previous pastor's moral failure, the congregation was embroiled in a multimillion dollar lawsuit over a church discipline case. In the year between my predecessor's resignation and my arrival, the church lost hundreds of attendees and experienced severe reductions in the budget. At the ripe age of thirty, I was in way over my head.

The second church knew the privilege of a faithful, Bible-loving senior pastor who served the congregation as their only pastor for forty years. I had the challenge—and pleasure—of being the guy to follow in his footsteps. (This gracious leader stayed in the church supporting me the entire eleven years of my pastoral ministry.) Despite being "the rookie" showing up after this seasoned pro, God did a profound work in this northern California church. We saw significant renewal and growth as the church planted daughter congregations and increased our impact literally around the world. The highlight of that assignment was a powerful prayer movement that sparked transformation in thousands of lives, launched several national conferences, and eventually led to the formation of the organization I lead today, Strategic Renewal.

The third assignment was the toughest. A congregation in the Midwest had relocated to a new campus in 2002. On their sixty-two acres they built a large, beautiful facility that included a worship center seating more than four thousand. In spite of the generosity of the congregation toward this project, a devalued U.S. stock market following the 9/11 terrorist attacks of 2001 left many unable to fulfill their pledges. The church was left with a multimillion dollar mortgage and $10 million short in their cash campaign for the building. Then, only a few weeks after moving into the new facility, church members were jolted by the revelation that their enterprising pastor of fifteen years was engaged in an extramarital affair. The people were devastated.

About a year later, I was called as the next pastor of this hurting megachurch. Again, God's work of spiritual renewal saved the day as we faithfully taught His Word and aggressively sought Him on our knees. The Lord was so gracious to us. Today I have the joy of returning a couple times a year for ministry, and visiting my dear and faithful friends, since the church supports me as one of their missionaries. They are growing again under the leadership of their new pastor.

Lessons from the Black Box

In both the first and last assignments, I came into a situation where I had to analyze and deal with the "black box" of a leadership failure. By God's grace, I had to discern the cause and effects of an embarrassing and hurtful crash. There were lessons to learn here—lessons about brokenness, grace, prayer, determination, and restoration.

There were also lessons to learn about leadership. Just as the "black box" on a plane will help you understand what went wrong, so the task of sorting through the ashes of a leadership failure provides powerful lessons about keeping other leaders in the air. A few observations stand out:

- *Most leaders stay in flight in spite of the difficulties.* It is a point of optimism and gratitude that most leaders fly straight and end well. For every story of a leadership disaster, there are hundreds of faithful Christian leaders who serve with honor and humility every day. They strive to walk with Christ, love their spouses, care for their families, and faithfully lead those entrusted to their care.
- *No flight plan expects to end in disaster.* Good men and women, seeking to obey the call of God and make a difference in this world, begin this leadership journey every day. They want to fly and finish respectably. Unfortunately, storms and stresses begin to take a toll. Improper self-management takes them off course. Over time, leaders can find themselves in places of discouragement and defeat they never imagined would occur.

- *Many leaders don't realize when they are in trouble.* In recent decades, larger aircraft have been required to utilize a piece of equipment called the ground proximity warning system (GPWS). When planes get too close to the ground or the surrounding terrain, the system provides instructions for evasive maneuvers such as "Terrain! Terrain! Pull up! . . ." along with a warning horn. This equipment has dramatically reduced the number of accidents for planes flying over unfamiliar terrain, or too close to the ground.

  God has provided a kind of GPWS for leaders. It is the voice of conscience, which alerts us to issues of moral compromise. But over time human beings can become dull to this voice. Many who crash are in a pattern of self-deception, flying entirely without that objective sense of how close to the ground they really are. This, again, is where objective input and the right leadership "instruments" are vital.

- *God has provided everything a leader needs to stay in flight and land the leadership plane successfully.* This book is really not about leadership crashes but leadership success. The key is the commitment of a leader to utilize the "instrument panel" and the related warning systems through which the sufficiency of the Word of God, the Spirit of God, and the people of God can flow into the very being of a leader to keep him in flight and on course for the good of the passengers and the glory of God.

- *Leaders who experience and tolerate spiritual disorientation will crash and burn.* Just as skilled, intelligent, experienced pilots flying sophisticated aircraft can become disoriented, so leaders can unintentionally get into a situation where up seems down, left seems right, and backward seems forward. Understanding the dynamics of disorientation then learning how to avoid it is vital for the leader who wants to soar. For a leader already caught in a subjective downward spiral, a dose of encouraging objectivity with a fresh vision of the "instruments" is a matter of ministry life or death.

No leader ever wants to be in a situation where he is holding the black box of a previous disaster. The pain of dealing with wounded people, shattered dreams, and devastated relationships is overwhelming. Yet, amid the rubble, God is good to instruct, heal, and restore hope.

Peter, Paul, and Learning to Soar

Of course, the greater reality is that God has given every leader everything necessary to truly soar in their influence and example. Peter, a flawed leader who was restored and empowered by the truth and Spirit of God, wrote to remind us of Christ's sufficiency for our calling: "His divine power has given to us all things that pertain to life and godliness, through the knowledge of Him who called us by glory and virtue, by which have been given to us exceedingly great and precious promises, that through these you may be partakers of the divine nature, having escaped the corruption that is in the world through lust" (2 Peter 1:3–4).

As we will see, Paul understood the reality of leadership storms. In Romans 8 he spoke of tribulation, distress, persecution, famine, nakedness, peril, and even the sword, or the threat of death through martyrdom. Quoting from the Old Testament, he testified that we are "accounted as sheep for the slaughter" (Romans 8:36). These were realistic expectations for Christ-followers in the first century, and especially for leaders. Yet, he gives us this powerful promise, "In all these things we are more than conquerors through Him who loved us" (Romans 8:37).

One thing I appreciate about the apostle Paul is the way in which he always kept expectations realistic for his followers. He warned them of suffering and tribulation as an essential part of the journey.

In following the sacrificial model of his Savior, Paul became very familiar with the trials and perils of genuine discipleship and leadership. Even in the moments surrounding his conversion and calling, Jesus would reveal to him "how many things he must suffer for My name's sake" (Acts 9:16). Throughout his leadership he faced persecution, mockery, and threats of death.

It comes as no surprise when Paul pours his heart out to his son in the faith, Timothy, that he reminds him of the sufferings of discipleship and the storms of leadership. In his final and very personal leadership letter to Timothy, he writes, "I also suffer these things; nevertheless I am not ashamed, for I know whom I have believed and am persuaded that He is able to keep what I have committed to Him until that Day" (see 2 Timothy 1:12). Speaking extensively again of this suffering and afflictions, he reminds Timothy and all of us of the reality that "all who desire to live godly in Christ Jesus will suffer persecution" (2 Timothy 3:12).

Of course, Paul gives a reality check in this last letter of his life as he warns leaders of the "perilous times" ahead. Using some metaphors from his own day, he urges his disciple to remain unencumbered like a dedicated soldier, play by the rules like a winning athlete, and expect a harvest like a faithful farmer (2 Timothy 2:1–7). Of course, planes and pilots did not exist in Paul's day, but I can almost hear him also say, "Endure unexpected storms like a skilled pilot."

Paul understood the risks and responsibilities of an enduring leader. He passed these perspectives on to Timothy with clarity and honesty. When we embrace these truths, we are able to defy gravity and become effective leaders.

Keys to Survive and Thrive

Let's learn the vital lessons from Paul that will help us soar in the leadership flights of our lives. Remember that Paul was speaking to a young man rattled by fear in the face of leadership challenges. He told Timothy not to give in to fear but to focus on power, love, and self-discipline.

But note the *final* advice Paul ever gave to anyone in recorded Scripture. He spoke it in the same breath in which he referred to his imminent death. Not only was it the key to Timothy's leadership performance but it is pivotal to our navigation of leadership storms: "As for you, be calm and cool and steady, accept and suffer unflinchingly every hardship, do the work of an evangelist, fully perform all the duties of your ministry" (2 Timothy 4:5 AMP). The New Living Translation reads: "But you should keep a clear mind in every situation. Don't be afraid of suffering for the Lord. Work at telling others the Good News, and fully carry out the ministry God has given you."

So here it is. If we are going to defy gravity and soar above the unexpected storms of leadership, it is imperative to keep a calm, clear, and steady perspective as we endure the certain suffering of the call. We must keep on course. We must be faithful to the mission assigned to us. We must complete the flight safely. Paul did. As he said, "I have fought the good fight, I have finished the race, I have kept the faith" (2 Timothy 4:7).

Paul finished his leadership flight. He endured incredible storms. He safely landed the plane. He was passionate to help us do the same.

The Discipline of Successful Flying

At 7:52 the morning of May 20, 1927, Charles A. Lindbergh took off in his single-engine plane, the *Spirit of St. Louis*, from Roosevelt Field near New York City. Flying northeast along the coast, he traversed Nova Scotia and Newfoundland before heading across the Atlantic Ocean, attempting history's first successful trans-Atlantic flight.

Lindbergh's attempt captured the imagination of the public like few events in history. Americans waited nervously by their radios, listening for news of the flight. Thirty-four hours after his departure from New York, a frenzied crowd of 150,000 people cheered his landing at Le Bourget Field in Paris.[1]

In a personal account of a crucial moment in his epic journey, Lindbergh wrote about his encounter with a potential storm:

A pillar of clouds block out the stars ahead, spilling over on top like a huge mushroom in the sky. . . . In the seconds that intervene while I approach, I make the mental and physical preparation for blind flying. The body must be informed sternly that the mind will take complete control. The senses must be drafted and lined up in the strictest discipline, while logic replaces instinct as commander. . . . The muscles must obey the mind's decision no matter how wrong it seems to them. If the eyes imagine the flicker of a star below where they think the horizon ought to be, if the ears report the engine's tempo too slow for level flight, if the nerves say the seat back's pressure is increasing (as it does in a climb), the hand and the feet must still be loyal to the order of the mind. It is a terrific strain on the mind also when it turns from long-proven bodily instincts to the cold, mechanical impartiality of needles moving over dials.

Then, using language almost reminiscent of the advice of the apostle Paul, Lindbergh offers a word of warning to those of us who intend to survive physical—and emotional—storms:

> If the senses get excited and out of control, the plane will follow them, and that can be fatal. If the senses break rank while everything is going right, it may be impossible, with the plane falling dizzily and needles running wild, to bring them back into line, reinstruct them, and force them to gain control while everything is going wrong. It would be like rallying a panicked army under the fire of an advancing enemy. Like an army under fire, blind flying requires absolute discipline. This must be fully understood before it starts.[2]

In aviation and in Christian leadership, storms are inevitable. Survival is not guaranteed, but it's highly probable for those who are prepared, those who keep their eyes on the instruments and trust the things they know to be true. As Christian leaders, we can trust those truths given to us by the One who called us—who in every way will help us *soar*.

*Your feelings cannot be trusted as the final authority on
what the airplane is doing. Your mind is boss. The
instruments are your window on reality, and you
desperately need to understand the data they provide. . . .
Our feelings, indulged without examination, will kill us.*

ERIC NOLTE
Commercial pilot, flight instructor, and author

*Lean on, trust in, and be confident
in the Lord with all your heart and mind and
do not rely on your own insight or understanding.*

PROVERBS 3:5 (AMP)

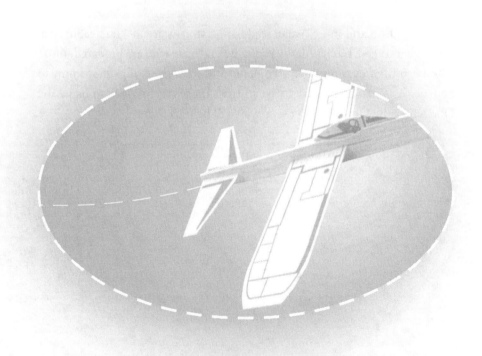

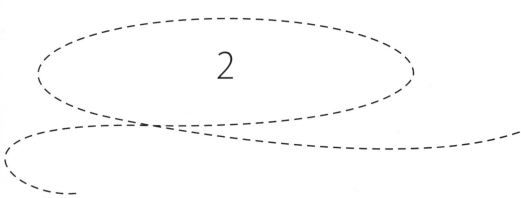

2

Trusting the Leadership Instruments

Essex County Airport in Fairfield, New Jersey, is a popular location for private pilots flying to or from New York City, which is just twenty miles east. On Friday night, July 16, 1999, Kyle Bailey was preparing to take off from Essex County Airport—but he changed his mind. Several other pilots also canceled flights that night because of adverse visual conditions.

"I was planning on going to Martha's Vineyard last night too," said Bailey, "but it was so hazy. I'm very cautious, though. And I'm not crazy about flying over water at night."

Kyle Bailey was the last person to talk to John F. Kennedy Jr. that night, just before Kennedy, his wife, Carolyn, and his sister-in-law, Lauren Bissette, took off in his Piper Saratoga. The Kennedys were eventually flying to Hyannis, Massachusetts, for a Saturday family wedding but planned to drop off Lauren at Martha's Vineyard on the way.

Kyle Bailey noticed Kennedy limping as he got ready to make the flight that Friday night. JFK Jr. had broken his foot the previous month when he flew his paraglider into a tree. The break kept him from flying solo all summer long—until that Friday night.

Bailey told reporters, "He had at least one crutch. I saw him limping. I told my family, 'I can't believe he's going up in this weather.'"[1] But Kennedy did go up. And his plane crashed into the Atlantic Ocean.

Experts with the National Transportation Safety Board (NTSB) believe that Kennedy's plane went into what is known as a "graveyard spiral," the most dangerous and deadly of airplane spins. In a graveyard spiral, a plane locks into a tight turn, and then accelerates rapidly, with the nose of the plane pointed straight down. Investigators concluded Kennedy's aircraft impacted the water inverted and at high speed.

In the wake of this disaster, many have speculated about the causes of Kennedy's disastrous flight. Some point to the foot injury, since the Saratoga utilizes foot pedals for guiding the plane. Others note that Kennedy was reluctant to even fly to Martha's Vineyard that night, but felt pressure from his wife to do so in order to drop off her sister, Lauren. Pilots flying similar routes on the night of the accident told the NTSB no visual horizon existed while flying over the water because of haze. Ultimately, the accident was the result of spatial disorientation, spurred by the haze (poor visibility), and the night sky.[2]

Kennedy had not yet completed his instrument certification, which would have been essential in inclement weather. It is probable that Kennedy became confused and began controlling the plane himself. Without the ability to use the more sophisticated instruments, he was overtaken by spatial disorientation, which resulted in the fatal graveyard spin.

Leadership Vertigo

Many Christian leaders are "losing altitude" in ways that most of us do not see or understand. When we "suddenly" hear of a respected executive in our church whose marriage has disintegrated, or a well-known pastor caught in moral indiscretion, we should remember these "crashes" are usually the result of numerous bad decisions made during a long, downward emotional, mental, and spiritual spiral. Sometimes the leader was seeking help during his descent toward disaster. Often it was concealed to everyone.

Recently I was leading an areawide prayer event in a major North Carolina city. During an afternoon session, several pastors opened up for the first time about their debilitating battles with discouragement. As each one prayed, with tears, about their emotional struggle to even "hang in there," the other men in their small groups were surprised. Two of the pastors were best friends, working and meeting together regularly in shared community efforts. As they prayed for one another, each one revealed that he had no idea that the other one was so disheartened. Leaders tend to conceal their cockpit consternation pretty well, often leading to isolation, and sometimes their eventual demise.

Biblical Leaders in Downward Drift

The Old Testament does not disguise the emotional struggles of Israel's great leaders. We read about Moses losing altitude when he became overwhelmed with the monumental task of leading God's complaining people. He asked God to kill him and put him out of his misery (Numbers 11:15). The first king of Israel, the strong and impressive King Saul, lost altitude when he became jealous toward the young and popular David (1 Samuel 18:9–12).

More than once, David, the anointed future king, lost altitude from weariness over running from Saul. On one occasion he fled to a Philistine city. Afraid for his life, he pretended to be insane, slobbering on himself and scratching the walls in a ploy to survive. On another occasion, he fled again to a Philistine city where he made an alliance with these enemy armies, which led to deeper complexity and disaster (1 Samuel 27:1). Leaders losing altitude can behave strangely and irrationally.

Even the prophet Elijah, the recipient of God's direct revelation, lost altitude after an intense confrontation with the prophets of Baal at Mt. Carmel. Alone in the wilderness, deeply fatigued and coping with the threats on his life by Queen Jezebel, he prayed that God would let him just die (1 Kings 19:4).

In the New Testament, the apostle Paul at one point gave up hope of survival in the face of the severe trials in the province of Asia (2 Corinthians 1:8). Similarly, the young leader Timothy lost altitude when he was overtaken by fear amid the spiritual challenges of leading the church at Ephesus

(2 Timothy 1:7). Demas, a trusted associate of the apostle Paul, lost altitude when he began to fall in love with the things of the world. Eventually he completely self-destructed, abandoning his ministry (2 Timothy 4:10).

These are just a few of the many stories that remind us of the vulnerability great leaders can experience during the storms of ministry and the pressures of responsibility. This kind of spiritual vertigo is nothing new to human leadership. Everyone in leadership, modern and ancient, proves faulty and susceptible to the downward spiral.

Trained to Trust

When pilots are preparing for their instrument rating, instructors go to great lengths to train them to thoroughly understand and trust the instruments. One instructional manual describes one way of focusing prospective pilots on their cockpit instruments: "Most of your time in the airplane will be accomplished using a view limiting device. This device restricts your view of outside the airplane so you maintain reference only to the cockpit instruments." Even though the pilot-in-training is flying on a clear day, this view restricting device forces him to see nothing but the instruments. Of course, it is counterintuitive to do so, but it really becomes a matter of life and death once the pilot is in actual flight.

The Physiology of Flight

Textbooks for flight students and aspiring pilots address the physical challenges of flight with great detail and candor. They call these the "human factors" of flight and note that human factors account for over 80 percent of all accidents. One textbook published by the Federal Aviation Administration warns that flying in poor conditions can "result in sensations that are misleading to the body's sensory system. A safe pilot needs to understand these sensations and effectively counteract them."[3]

Textbooks on flying typically address three of the body's sensory systems: the visual (eyes), the vestibular (ears), and the postural (nerves). The effectiveness and complexity of these systems are a testament to God's profound creative work. Each is essential to safe flight. Yet the three systems are fallible. This unreliability leads to disaster if a pilot is not keenly aware of aviation physiology and resolute in managing each physical system with great care.

Disorientation That Can Lead to Disaster

During flight in "visual meteorological conditions" (clear visibility), the pilot's eyes are a primary orientation source that usually provide accurate and reliable input. As one training manual states, "When these visual cues are taken away, false sensations can cause the pilot to become disoriented."[4] The pilot's inner ear and nerves can send confusing signals. When the sense of balance is off, it is called *vestibular disorientation*. When the nervous system becomes confused, it is known as *spatial disorientation*.

This disorientation can cause a pilot to overcompensate for perceived plane-control problems in ways that can endanger the pilot and passengers. The worst of these confused attempts leads to "graveyard spiral," where the plane dives rapidly in a circular pattern. The pilot is usually completely confused about what is going on prior to the resulting crash.

Pilots actually practice controlled maneuvers during their flight training to gain a comprehensive understanding of this danger of disorientation. They must learn through these training experiences about their own susceptibility to disorientation—and that their subjective judgments about the direction, pitch, and turn of their aircraft based on bodily sensations are frequently false. All of this leads to a greater confidence in relying on the flight instruments rather than their own subjective sensations.

In What Do We Trust?

The task of leadership has several fascinating parallels to the task of flying a plane. Just as a pilot's vision can be restricted by poor weather or unusual conditions, so a leader's perception of a given situation can be limited and flawed. Just as the physiology of the inner ear can become confused, so a leader's inner voice can give input that is confusing and erroneous. And just as a pilot's nervous system can misinterpret the environment, so a leader's emotions can create subjective scenarios that lead to bad decisions.

Trusting our flawed perceptions, our confused internal conversations, and our wide range of emotions feels natural, but is ultimately perilous.

Let's see how each of these faulty guides can confuse us as leaders.

1. Flawed Perceptions

Two people can have a very different perception of a situation. In recent years marketers have sold special pictures that present a multicolored image with a second subliminal character carefully camouflaged in the design. Stare at the picture for a few seconds with just the right focus, and the second image typically will emerge. Most people can see the hidden images with ease, but not everyone. Similarly, if you can't see the storms, you're in trouble. When we fail to utilize the leadership instruments (introduced at the end of this chapter and taught in detail in part 2), we can easily operate with very limited perception.

2. Internal Conversation

Every person engages in an ongoing internal dialogue, what some call *self-talk*. These internal conversations are what drive a person's emotions and actions. It is imperative that these self-conversations are truthful. But sometimes we give faulty messages to ourselves. Self-deception inevitably results.

Jeremiah's familiar description reminds us of the danger of trusting in the subjective reasoning of our own heart: "The heart is deceitful above all things, and desperately wicked; who can know it?" (Jeremiah 17:9). Enduring leaders learn to carefully evaluate the internal words of the heart and to submit these conversations to the objective wisdom of God. There is a real sense in which the most dangerous lies we tell are the ones we tell ourselves.

Parallels between Flying and Leading

Flying	Leading
Flying	**Leading**
1. The eyes: Susceptible to optical illusions	1. Perception: Possible misinterpretation of events
2. The inner ear: Vulnerable to vertigo	2. The inner voice: Internal conversations that are untrue
3. The nerves: At risk of disorientation	3. The emotions: Subjective reactions to events

3. Our Emotions

Even great leaders can be overcome by mistaken perceptions, confused self-talk, and vulnerable emotions to the point of spiritual and functional disorientation. What we need, according to author Samuel Rima, is "emotional self-leadership." He warns, "When we consistently interpret events through a subjective mental grid that tends to distort reality, our subjectivity will result in distorted emotions. . . . If we are ever going to fulfill our calling and achieve our life goals we will be required to learn how to master our emotions so that they do not end up mastering us." Rima concludes that our internal emotions in large measure "determine who we are and what we become."[5]

One evening many years ago while meeting with a group of elders, I saw the power of internal emotions to mislead us. A man was suing the church over an incident that had occurred prior to my arrival. The church had disciplined the man for factious behavior. He, in turn, sued them for $25 million dollars to vindicate himself. Because he was independently wealthy, he was able to bankroll his legal case. The situation had been at an impasse for over five years.

After hours of circular conversation and heated disagreements in the ex-member's living room, one of the elders stood up in profound exasperation and stormed out of the house. This elder was a respected high school principal, usually even-tempered and characteristically self-controlled. In speaking with him later, he humbly confessed, "Emotions have no brains." This is so true. He could not deal with the man's adversarial stance and, out of control, got up, walked to the door, and exited to his car.

Choosing to Trust the Instruments

Do you see the need for objective instruments as a leader? Most pilots do. One popular textbook for pilots tells of the early airmail planes with limited navigation equipment, flown during an era when weather information often was unavailable. Of the first forty aviators hired to fly the mail, thirty-one were killed while flying.[6]

Were these thirty-one mail delivery pilots less intelligent or sincere than pilots today? Of course not. Were they kamikazes? No way. Were they less skilled than other pilots? Likely not. Rather, they were flying without proper objective instruments. The thirty-one pilots succumbed to visual limitations, spatial disorientation, and subjective decision making that led to their death. It is a very sad reality. Their planes were not equipped with the proper instruments and navigation equipment to allow pilots to safely fly in the clouds or in low visibility conditions.

This same classic textbook provides statistics that demonstrate that the risk of weather-related accidents declines as pilots gain instrument flying experience. Pilots with less than fifty hours of instrument time were involved in 58 percent of all weather accidents and 47 percent of fatal weather accidents. As pilots gain more experience (fifty to one hundred hours of instrument flying time), their risk decreases to slightly below 9 percent of all accidents.[7]

Your Leadership Instrument Panel

So what instruments do we need to lift off and climb above the storms when they come? In the pages to follow, you will be introduced to a "leadership instrument panel" that presents nine vital areas of concern for the enduring leader. As leaders encounter the storms, these gauges will provide vital input to prevent subjective sabotage and to ensure a successful leadership flight. Our leadership instrument panel has nine gauges:

1. Applied Truth
2. Spiritual Intimacy
3. Personal Integrity
4. Biblical Identity
5. Genuine Accountability
6. Eternal Significance
7. Healthy Family Life
8. Indispensable Pain
9. A Captivating Call

Each chapter will include words from Christian leaders who have faced incredible storms. You'll read about pastors, business executives, mission leaders, athletes, and entrepreneurs. These men and women speak honestly and compellingly about moments in their journey that made all the difference. Their testimonies affirm the power of the instrument panel.

Part 2
Viewing the Leadership Instrument Panel

The doctrines of Scripture are facts, which involve corresponding emotions and principles of action, and must, from their very nature, if believed, be operative upon the heart and the life. If the doctrines of Scripture exert no godly influence, carry with them no practical weight, exert no moral power, they are not truly believed.

JOHN ANGELL JAMES
English pastor and writer

I suffer trouble as an evildoer, even to the point of chains; but the word of God is not chained.

2 TIMOTHY 2:9

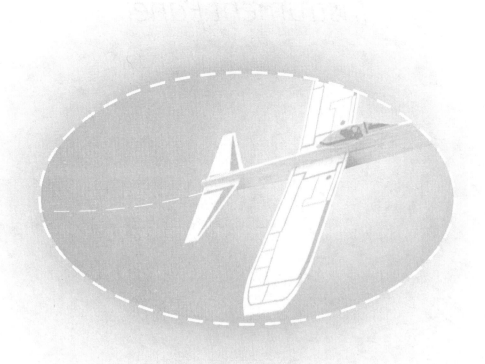

3

Gauge One:

Applied Truth

Early in his ministry, Pastor John MacArthur walked into a staff meeting one Tuesday morning eager to express his deep appreciation for the support and collegial friendships he was enjoying with this pastoral staff. This team of six young men had been of great help to him as he was establishing his leadership at Grace Community Church in Sun Valley, California. The church was flourishing. These men had served together, prayed together, studied together, and played basketball together. From John's perspective, this team was the heart and soul of his effectiveness in the work.

What occurred in that morning staff meeting would be tagged for years to come as "Black Tuesday." Rather than reciprocate Pastor John's appreciation, the de facto leader of the group responded, essentially, "If you think we're your friends, you have another think coming." As John describes it, a full-blown mutiny took place on the spot.

"I was devastated," he recalls. "These were the only guys I had. But they had conferred together to conclude that I was too dominant and did not share preaching with them. They stated their intention to take their grievance to the elders' meeting later that week. It was probably the all-time low point of my ministry."

In time Pastor John survived the crisis with the support of the elders. Each one of these young leaders left the church, and all but one left ministry permanently. Eventually each reconciled with Pastor John. But at the time he felt devastated.

"This was my best shot as a young pastor at investing in people, and I experienced a 180 degree turn in the wrong direction. I suddenly realized I did not have anybody to count on or work with. It was a true 2 Corinthians 12 experience where God allowed a stake to be driven through my heart to keep me from exalting myself."[1]

During that time Pastor MacArthur found great strength in his resolute and systematic study of the Scriptures. "I took my rest in the fact that God would honor His Word," he recalls. "Whatever my failures and weaknesses were, I still knew how to study, interpret, and exposit the Bible. That is what God promised to bless. So I just kept going—digging into the Word and waiting on God. Isaiah 55:11 promised that His Word will never return void."[2] Forty years later, Pastor MacArthur still leads Grace Community Church, ministering to thousands each week through his systematic exposition of the Scriptures. Through his radio ministry, millions around the world have been enriched and equipped.

Like MacArthur, every leader encounters deep disappointments, hurts, and setbacks. Some eventually lose altitude and crash for lack of the powerful and objective guidance and strength of God's Word. Others learn to trust in the things that are true, reliable, and authoritative as revealed in the Bible. They succeed by defying gravity through the objective power of applied truth.

The Hope and Help of the Scriptures

Biblical leaders boldly affirm the powerful encouragement and endurance they receive from the truths of God's Word, found in both the Old and New Testaments.

We are all familiar with the severe trials and perplexities Job encountered. In the midst of his pain, Job affirmed his source of strength, "I have not departed from the commandment of His lips; I have treasured the words of His mouth more than my necessary food" (Job 23:12). For Job, God's commands were both a treasure and needed nourishment. Jeremiah, "the weeping prophet" who carried many burdens and endured harsh afflictions, still declared, "Your words were found, and I ate them, and Your word was to me the joy and rejoicing of my heart; For I am called by Your name, O Lord God of hosts" (Jeremiah 15:16). For Jeremiah, the Scriptures brought not only nourishment but joy. They affirmed his calling. For us as well, these are only a few of the powerful benefits of the truth.

Hope and healing always flow from the power of God's Word to the heart of a leader. Over and over in Psalm 119, the writer affirms the practical help of scriptural guidance with words like, "I rise before the dawning of the morning, and cry for help; I hope in Your word. . . . You are my hiding place and my shield; I hope in Your word" (Psalm 119:114, 147). Psalm 130:5 echoes the same conviction, "I wait for the Lord, my soul waits, and in His word I do hope." Psalm 107:20 speaks of the sinful rebellion of Israel in the desert but then declares, "He sent His word and healed them, and delivered them from their destructions."

The New Testament speaks often of the effectiveness of the Scriptures to work powerfully in our lives (1 Thessalonians 2:13) by transforming our minds (Romans 12:2), giving us hope (Romans 15:4), revealing our deepest issues (Hebrews 4:12), correcting wrong thoughts (Titus 1:9), causing us to grow (1 Peter 2:2), and keeping us strong (1 John 2:14). Second Timothy 3:16 offers encouragement to leaders with the promise that the Word is "profitable for doctrine, for reproof, for correction, for instruction in righteousness." All of these benefits are most powerful when they first work deeply in the heart.

Paul Powers, a skilled leader, Bible teacher, and pastor from Vermont, tells of his own commitment to embrace the hope of the Scriptures. Several years ago Powers wanted to leave the ministry and was suffering from clinical depression. The church leadership sent Paul and his wife to a retreat center to receive specialized counseling. Powers comments, "I knew I needed more help than I had already gotten. Through our counseling I found out I was still 'highly depressed.' I asked the counselor, 'If I am highly depressed now, how did I ever function before I got "better"?' His answer was insightful and has helped me since then. He responded, 'You are a highly disciplined person; so you have functioned out of sheer discipline.'"[3]

At first, Powers found this difficult to believe. But as he later processed these words and prayed about them, God showed him that it was the discipline of studying and getting into God's Word that helped him survive. He notes, "Since that time, when I have started to struggle, I try to get into the Word as soon as possible. I have proven repeatedly in the last year the truth of Romans 15:4 (NIV), 'that through the endurance and encouragement of the Scriptures we might have hope.'"

Every leader who has entrusted his soul to the staying power of the Scriptures during severe trials can joyously affirm the sentiments of Psalm 19:10–11 that the truths of God are to be desired more than gold, "yea, than much fine gold; sweeter also than honey and the honeycomb. Moreover by them Your servant is warned, and in keeping them there is great reward." Just as a pilot navigating severe storms keeps an eye on his instruments, so a wise leader looks intently to God's truth. To defy gravity, leaders become familiar with the great rewards of strength, wisdom, joy, direction, courage, and hope that spring from the Scriptures.

Inspired by Biblical Examples

Hans Finzel, president of the missions agency World Venture (formerly CB International), reflects on a recent season of his leadership when he was seeking to bring essential change to a sixty-five-year-old missions agency. As often happens, change agents are misunderstood and face doubts, resistance, and even questioning of motives. Finzel was under attack from board members, staff, and the broader constituency of the agency. "I was ready to leave. I had written my resignation letter. Already, I had spoken with the chairman of the board and a couple key staff members. I was so discouraged. But I would soon learn that God was not in it."[4]

Finzel describes a speaking assignment during that season that required him to study the life of Moses. Soon Finzel was deeply touched by the biblical example of Moses' seasons of discouragement, his fickle followers, and the many delays and detours in the journey to the Promised Land. He even observed the ways in which Moses was a cultural misfit compared to his followers, which related to Finzel's feelings about his own fit at times. He concluded that the only reason Moses did not quit was his relationship with God. He describes it in these terms, "Moses held my hand during those dark days. I concluded that if he could hang in there, then so could I. And the most fruitful days of our ministry have occurred since that personal wilderness when I was helped by God's Word and the life of Moses."[5]

The gauge of objective truth found in God's Word has many ways of helping us stay on course in our leadership flight. Sometimes it is a topical study. Other times, a particular Bible book or even one key verse may grip our hearts and renew our minds. The key is to fully engage with the prescription God gave Joshua to "meditate in it day and night" that we might "observe to do according to all that is written in it." Then we will make our "way prosperous, and then [we] will have good success" (Joshua 1:8). The promise is familiar, but still potent.

Climbing out of the Truthless Tailspin

Still, we have to be honest and admit that most Christian leaders who have experienced a disastrous crash have not lacked Bible knowledge. Some of the nation's greatest preachers have produced the most disconcerting scandals. Clearly, *it is not mere Bible knowledge* that produces the power to stay on course and in flight. Rather, *it is a consistent and authentic application of the knowledge* to the mind, heart, and life. Even Christian leaders can become "hearers" rather than "doers" and deceive their own hearts (see James 1:22–24) as they sit among the commentaries and study tools of their Christian library.

As a pastor for almost thirty years, I have had my share of "dry" seasons where I've been going through the motions—staring at the gauge of truth and feeling like it is not helping me in my leadership flight. What do we do to keep our interaction with God's revelation to our hearts fresh and vibrant? Here are five ways to keep the gauge of objective truth at the right level.

1. Evaluate the Soil

All four Gospels present Jesus telling the story of the sower and the soil. Without getting into all of the meanings and application, we can agree on the basic principle that quality soil is essential to spiritual fruit, springing from the seed of God's Word. We are challenged by the words, "and the cares of this world, the deceitfulness of riches, and the desires for other things [enter in to] choke the word, [so that] it becomes unfruitful" (Mark 4:19-20).

What was once fertile and had the potential of bearing fruit thirtyfold becomes unfruitful because of a misguided focus of the heart. I believe for a Christian leader, the "cares," "deceitfulness," and "desires" that damage the fertile soil of the soul are issues like busyness, distraction, fatigue, overwork, and hurry. Soon these manifest in neglect as we superficially interact with the truth. We are losing altitude, as the gauge of truth has been clouded over by a driven, disheveled life.

2. Recalibrate Spiritual Hunger

When our soil inspection reveals these troubles, we need to recalibrate to stimulate spiritual hunger. One way to create hunger is through periodic retreats that include several days of solitude, silence, fasting, prayer, and massive doses of reading. During my years as a pastor, I would do this two times annually—and with profound impact. Another way to stimulate hunger is to take a sabbatical of multiple weeks or months.

I have found that spiritual hunger and physical hunger are opposites. Physically when you are hungry and you eat, you become satisfied, or "full" as we say it. When you are hungry and you do not eat, you become hungrier (and probably grumpy). Spiritually, however, it works in reverse. When you are spiritually hungry and you eat, your appetite increases. When you are spiritually hungry and you don't eat, you become satisfied and the passion for the Word wanes.

That is why we sometimes need a recalibration where we get away and just "feast." I have found this is a powerful means of clearing my vision of the truth gauge and reengaging my heart, not just my mind, in the delight of applying truth to my life. Sometimes we need to just "stop the train" and jump into the Word.

3. Embrace Truth as More than a "Tool of the Trade"

Those in full-time vocational service can easily be "in the Word" without the Word being in them. The Bible simply becomes a means to the end of saying something witty and insightful at the next event or church service. But in the long run, the *process* is much more important than the *product*. It is the process of "labor[ing] in word and doctrine" (1 Timothy 5:17) that shapes character, out of which a life-changing message flows.

I've kept a plaque on my desk for many years that says, "God's Word sets me on fire and people come to see me burn" (apparently attributed to John Wesley). I have also reminded myself of God's word to Ezekiel, "Son of man, let all my words sink deep into your own heart first. Listen to them carefully for yourself. Then go to your people . . ." (Ezekiel 3:10–11a NLT). God's Word must work in us before it can work in others. We've heard the adage many times, "A sermon prepared in the mind reaches minds. A sermon prepared in the heart reaches hearts. A sermon prepared in the life reaches lives."

4. Welcome Evaluation

To remain engaged with God's Word, we need the honest and consistent inquiry of a few close friends, according to Finzel. "We all need some friends who will question, prod, and encourage us in our consistency in staying in God's Word," Finzel noted during a conversation on this subject. "Sometimes it is hard for a wife to rebuke a husband for his waning godliness— but some loving and strong friends can get in our face. I have even found that my grown children inspire me with their love for God's Word and are free to ask me about mine."[6]

5. Choose God's Word above Human Emotions

During my early thirties as I was trying to stabilize the congregation that had been rocked by the moral failure of the previous pastor, my wife and I experienced a lot of pain. As we say, "hurting people hurt others." We had to absorb much of the emotional trauma of the situation; it was so difficult that we almost left vocational ministry.

These hurting people sometimes wrote horrible letters. One group tried (unsuccessfully) to remove the pastoral staff and elders of the church. One day, we even came home from vacation to find a pornographic postcard in the mail. On the back some anonymous woman had written, "Dear Pastor Daniel—I sure enjoyed our time together the other night. Let's get together again soon. Love, S—." My wife concluded that S stood for Satan. Of course, on top of all this we were trying to deal with the multimillion-dollar lawsuit and to stabilize the church.

During those days my sanity survived only by the truths found in the Scriptures: God is sovereign, God is good, and God is just. The whole situation felt very out of control, very bad, and very unfair. But I could choose what to believe and fix my heart on. Would it be my feelings, my circumstances, or what I *knew* to be true?

Yes, the whole ordeal felt very wrong. Yet I could focus on truths about who God is. His holy Word transcended the storm to tell me that He was in control (Psalm 46:10), He was good (Psalm 31:19), and He was just in all things (1 Peter 2:23). Without these truths, I would have crashed and burned.

Beyond the Academic to the Personal

Why do leaders sometimes lose sight of the sufficiency of the Scriptures as a source of encouragement and perspective? Pastor Powers believes it is because we let the Bible become academic and don't "hear" God speaking to us through it. His solution? "For the most part I have tried to 'feed myself' before I try to get truth to teach others. Over the years I have been encouraged by Acts 20:28, 'Therefore take heed to yourselves . . .' and 2 Timothy 2:6, 'The hardworking farmer must be first to partake of the crops.' Having grown up on a dairy farm in a family that was not rich, I knew the farm supplied all our basic needs."

Indeed, you don't have to be a farmer or a pastor to apply this truth: God's Word is powerful, able to meet our needs and keep us on course in the midst of inevitable storms of leadership. Like God Himself, the Scriptures are sufficient and powerful to help us defy gravity and climb above any storm.

Prayerlessness is my declaration
of independence from God.

DANIEL HENDERSON

In Your presence is fullness of joy.

PSALM 16:11

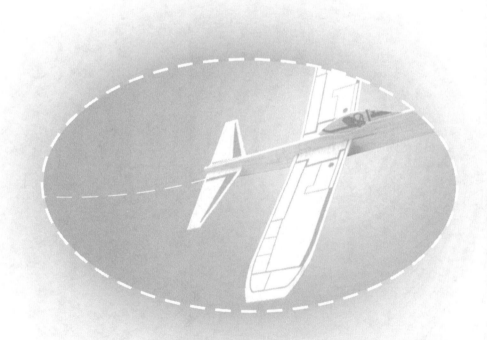

4

Gauge Two:

Spiritual Intimacy

Several times I've read about a leader who was losing altitude like a wounded duck. He was honest and sincere, but he was also wounded. He even doubted the value of his spiritual walk, and he questioned the goodness of God. He had observed the prosperity of godless people around him and had become bitter. Meanwhile, the incessant difficulties of people of faith disturbed him. His thoughts became so volatile that, had he given verbal expression to them, he would have been branded as a traitor to the faith.

Filled with negative emotion and deep questions, this leader knew he was in deep trouble.

But one day he experienced the presence of God. Everything changed. Clarity returned. Gratitude filled his heart again. He fell in love once more with his Creator and rebounded with powerful, practical hope.

I relate to this guy's story and have read it dozens of times. But, I do not know his name. He is only described as one of the "sons of Asaph" and his journey is captured in Psalm 73.

In the midst of a serious downward spiritual spiral, the psalmist's game-changer is found in verse 17, "Until I went into the sanctuary of God; then I understood . . ." This experience of God's presence turned his doubt into delight and his heartache into hunger. He concludes the psalm by declaring, "Whom have I in heaven but You? And there is none upon earth that I desire besides You. My flesh and my heart fail; But God is the strength of my heart and my portion forever. . . . It is good for me to draw near to God; I have put my trust in the Lord God, that I may declare all Your works" (Psalm 73:25–28).

Like this son of Asaph, twenty-first-century leaders can lose perspective and passion when they get their eyes off the "spiritual intimacy" gauge and look instead at the superficial circumstances of their life. We were made to enjoy God's presence and find our strength, peace, and perspective in the intimate connection available to us in Christ through prayer.

Powered by His Presence

I have read dozens of leadership books, yet I remain deeply impressed with pure biblical descriptions of every notable leader. Scripture presents a radically different idea about leadership compared to the ideas of many of our modern leadership gurus. Biblically, the common denominator of excellent leadership is found, not in personality, organizational technique, or refined people skills, but in the idea that "the Lord was with" each leader.

Certainly, every leader in Scripture had a mix of natural attributes and developed skills. However, the primary secret to their excellence was a genuine and manifest sense of the presence and power of God.[1] From Abraham to John the Baptist, this sense distinguished their impact. Today this factor sustains leaders who have a humble, enduring, and prayerful walk with God.

Throughout the Old Testament, the secret to high-impact leadership was the supernatural blessing of God. "The Lord was with" each one. This blessing was always directly linked to the heart attitudes of humility, obedience, and prayerfulness on the part of the leader. "For the eyes of the Lord run to and fro throughout the whole earth, to show Himself strong on behalf of those whose heart is loyal to Him" (2 Chronicles 16:9).

In His final words to His disciples, after telling them of their coming task to make disciples of all nations, Jesus gave one statement to empower and reassure His listeners. Jesus said, "*I am with you always*, even to the end of the age" (Matthew 28:20, italics added). Such power permeated the early church through the presence of the Holy Spirit, often in direct connection to prayer lives maintained by the spiritual leaders.[2]

Weapons of Mass Distraction

One particular Sunday as I finished preaching at a Virginia church, the senior pastor came to the pulpit to share his personal response to the message. He noted his ongoing battle with distraction. He called distraction a primary ploy of the Devil to make Christian leaders ineffective, particularly in reference to a vital prayer life. He described Satan's effort as "weapons of mass distraction."

In pondering that description, I have concluded that the Enemy does not have to destroy us but simply distract us. Little distractions tolerated over a long period of time result in big disasters.

I often tell Christian leaders that "the power of no is in a stronger yes." The ability to discard distractions is grounded in knowing—and choosing—the best priorities. We must embrace these priorities with a passionate yes in our hearts. And when distractions come, *no* becomes a positive Christian word—positive because it is rooted in strong convictions about the best and highest commitments.

Choosing one's priorities is a recurring theme in the Scriptures. The classic story, of course, involves the choices of Martha and Mary when Jesus came to visit. Busy and distracted, Martha became frustrated and critical in the moment. Her sister, Mary, embraced a clear yes as she prioritized seeking Christ over serving Christ. Jesus commended her for her focus as being the better choice and the one that would ultimately matter in eternity (Luke 10:38–42).

In Acts 6:1–7 the early apostles refused to get distracted with the broken program for feeding the widows. They directed a process of finding qualified and godly servants to solve the problem, but they would not compromise their own commitment to "prayer and to the ministry of the word." As a result, God blessed their focus with an unleashing of His power. The Word of God spread, the disciples multiplied greatly, and great numbers of hard-line Jewish priests were miraculously converted. There was no mass distraction among them.

In Exodus 18 we see an overwhelmed Moses. This great leader has become weary from judging the people. Now his astute father-in-law offers him some life-saving wisdom, recommending three priorities: Stand before God in prayer, teach the people the statutes and the laws, and delegate to other capable men the authority to judge the people at all times (vv. 19–21).

In both Acts 6 and Exodus 18, the first priority for unencumbered leadership was prayer. It is clear that this is a simple but profound defense against the Devil's weapons of mass distraction. This issue of intimacy with God is core to spiritual health and leadership survival.

Unbalanced Leadership

Jim Shaddix, senior pastor of Riverside Baptist Church in downtown Denver, Colorado, has written several books on preaching and has a growing radio ministry. He speaks openly of the constant battle to maintain the priority of spiritual intimacy in the midst of the storms and demands of leadership.

Early in his leadership journey, he was pastoring a church in Arlington, Texas. The young, growing congregation was able to build their first building just two years into his ministry. "We filled our small building within six months of occupancy and our growth immediately leveled out. But we couldn't even begin to think about building again due to our huge debt. I found myself in a panic trying to 'make' the church grow. Busyness, doubt, and low self-esteem all set in, leaving me with no motivation or desire to nurture my spiritual life."[3]

During that chapter of his ministry, he met with two seasoned pastors, both of whom had led prayer conferences at his church. "God used those two men to establish some disciplines in my life that had waned during this time of ministry frustration and challenges. Following those encounters, I met with our church leaders and asked them to help me maintain those priorities. Together, we established some guidelines and parameters for my ministry that would help me protect the practice of rising early in the morning to spend the first hours of my day in prayer."

Years later, Shaddix would serve in an academic environment where he was able to express his passion to help future leaders discover an intimate spiritual formation in prayer and the Scriptures. His life became very busy as the Lord extended his impact as a professor, itinerant preacher, and author. And that brought a different challenge. "How ironic it was when my academic pursuit and then subsequent busy ministry began to pull me away from the very thing that launched me on the journey!" Shaddix recalls. "I was traveling here and there to lead conferences and preach. My life got so busy and my schedule was so erratic. It was filled with 'spiritual' activity to the point that I found myself neglecting the very foundation of spiritual power." He notes, "Having to relearn lessons is often harder than having to learn them the first time."

Shaddix points to an unbalanced ministry as the battleground. "I know in my own life that one of the reasons for minimizing the role of prayer at different seasons in my ministry has been what I call an 'unbalanced' ministry. When I find myself neglecting prayer, it's usually not because of some blatant, unconfessed sin in my life, but due to my emphasis on some other part of ministry. For example, I eat, drink, and sleep expository preaching! Yet, Acts 6:4 says of the apostles that they gave themselves to 'prayer *and* to the ministry of the word.' It doesn't say they gave themselves to 'prayer *or* the ministry of the word.' There was no option. It was both—prayer and the ministry of the Word. But my passion for the ministry of the Word can sometime cause me to neglect prayer, creating an unbalanced ministry."[4]

Staying in the Supernatural Strike Zone

Every leader can relate to Jim's struggle and our constant battle with the things that distract us away from a genuine experience of spiritual intimacy. Conversely, when a leader is able to cultivate a deep intimacy with Christ, out of which everything else flows, he or she is in what I call the "supernatural strike zone." Indeed, the Lord is with this leader in an evident way because he is consistently with the Lord.

E. M. Bounds, a Civil War chaplain and pastor, wrote with great conviction and clarity about this supernatural strike zone of spiritual leadership. One of his quotes I have cherished for many years speaks of the vital priority of spiritual intimacy through prayer:

> Prayer cannot be retired as a secondary force in this world. To do so is to retire God from the movement. It is to make God secondary. The prayer ministry is an all-engaging force. It must be so to be a force at all. The estimate and place of prayer is the estimate and place of God. To give prayer the secondary place is to make God secondary in life's affairs. To substitute other forces of prayer retires God and materializes the whole movement.
>
> It is better to let the work go by default than to let the praying go by neglect. Whatever affects the intensity of our praying affects the value of our work. "Too busy to pray" is not only the keynote to backsliding, but it mars even the work done. Nothing is well done without prayer for the simple reason that it leaves God out of the account. It is so easy to be seduced by the good to neglect of the best, until both the good and the best perish. How easy to neglect prayer or abbreviate our praying simply by the plea that we have church work on our hands. Satan has effectively disarmed us when he can keep us too busy doing things to stop and pray.[5]

In my own pursuit to learn to pray, God has allowed me the privilege of leading multiple prayer experiences every week of my life for the past twenty-five years, including more than thirty-five Prayer Summits with various members of my congregations. These three-day events involve time away at a retreat center, with no agenda or speaker. Participants engage in spontaneous Scripture reading, singing, and prayerful response. We've gone away in groups ranging from 70 to 225. The results are truly life changing. While I am not a natural "prayer guy," my quest has been resolute. I always say that "God is glad to oblige when we give Him our undivided attention."

As you seek to watch the gauge of spiritual intimacy more passionately, I want to suggest four factors that have been enormously helpful for me.

1. Clarity about Why We Pray

The first marker on our gauge of spiritual intimacy is our motive for praying. Philosopher Friedrich Nietzsche noted that he who has a *why* can bear with almost any *how*. Our great battle in prayer is much more about motive than methodology. Jesus exposed the reality of misguided motives as He addressed the religious leaders of the day (see Matthew 6), exposing them as praying in order to be recognized as superspiritual. *I have learned that I can often do all the right things, but for all the wrong reasons.* My journey in prayer has certainly been a painful discovery of higher and holier motives.

If we are not careful, we can be motivated by mere guilt or duty in our prayers. "Acceptance" can also be a driver in our prayers as each of us desires to be seen as a "good Christian leader" who knows how to pray.

In our world where "bigger is always better," it is tempting to adopt prayer as the next and newest strategy for greater results in our business or ministry. It is difficult to extract our ego from the drive for organizational growth. When prayer does not succeed as a church growth tool or business advancement strategy, it is discarded for a more "effective" methodology. This explains why prayer tends to come and go in some churches and companies.

In my own progression toward a purer motive, I embraced the vision for revival as a primary focus in my prayers. As noble as this great need for a spiritual healing in our land is, I have come to realize that there is a difference between seeking revival from God and seeking God for revival.

One of my prayer mentors, Peter Lord, a pastor for more than forty years, wrote *The 29:59 Plan* (more than 600,000 copies sold).[6] One of the more insightful things Lord has told me is the basic truth that most Christians pray from either a grocery list or out of crisis. "Very few," he notes, "really understand the priority and passion to seek the face of God."

Accordingly, I have learned that the only enduring motive for prayer is that God is worthy to be sought. Since His worthiness will be the central focus of our worship and prayers in eternity, we are wise to make it the impetus to our prayers on earth. "You are worthy, O Lord, to receive glory and honor and power, for You created all things, and by Your will they exist and were created" (Revelation 4:11).

Over the years I have described this as "worship-based" prayer as compared to our common "request-based" prayers.[7] We should pray not as a duty but as a delight in the relationship with the one who is worthy of our love, our adoration, and our undivided attention.

2. Confession of Our Need to Pray

Not only must leaders learn that "He is worthy" as the primary impetus for prayer, but we must also learn to declare "I am needy" as the constant confession of the heart. Prayerlessness is a declaration of independence from God. A life that marginalizes prayer is a statement to God that His power is "optional" because we have strong confidence in our human ability to make it on our own.

Paul, one of the greatest leaders in Christian history, regularly declared his weakness. At the dawn of his Christian journey, sitting blind and bewildered in Damascus, it was said of him, "Behold he is praying." Not only do we see many examples of his prayer life in the letters he wrote, but we are given the heart behind this prayer commitment.

In his preaching, he intentionally embraced weakness, fear, and much trembling while refusing to rely on persuasive words of human wisdom. In doing so, he was going for a demonstration of the Spirit's power (1 Corinthians 2:3–4). He announced his own weakness and insufficiency, "And who is sufficient for these things?" (2 Corinthians 2:16). He learned a profound lesson through his personal struggle with a thorn in the flesh: "When I am weak, then I am strong" (2 Corinthians 12:10).

In Philippians 3:3 Paul declared he had "no confidence" in the flesh. In fact, he went on to describe his achievements, reiterating his "no confidence" attitude by describing his exploits as "rubbish" (Philippians 3:8).

Jim Cymbala, a pastor who leads with his eye on the gauge of spiritual intimacy both in his life and leadership as pastor of the Brooklyn Tabernacle, says it simply but profoundly, "God is attracted to weakness."

3. Community as Crucial to Prayer

The third prayer marker on the gauge of spiritual intimacy is the priority of community. Often at renewal events and pastors' conferences, I'm asked, "Which is more important, private prayer or corporate prayer?" My answer is always, "Yes!" It is like asking which leg is more crucial to walking. The right or the left?

Sadly, most leaders struggle to maintain a vibrant private prayer life. One primary reason is they do not understand the great encouragement and needful balance of praying regularly with others. I have learned that both are vital, practically and biblically.

Gene Getz, noted author, pastor, and retired seminary professor, teaches that the hallmark of Western civilization is rugged individualism. He boldly asserts that this "lens" has caused us to interpret the prayer passages of the New Testament as primarily personal in their application when, in the New Testament context, they were primarily applied in community. In his book *Praying for One Another*, he asks, "Why have we neglected the corporate emphasis on prayer found in Acts and the Epistles?" He then explains, "We use the personal pronouns 'I' and 'my' and 'me.' We have not been taught to think in terms of 'we' and 'our' and 'us.' Consequently, we individualize many references to corporate experience in the New Testament, thus often emphasizing personal prayer. More is said in Acts and the Epistles about corporate prayer, corporate learning of biblical truth, corporate evangelism, and corporate Christian maturity and growth than about the personal aspects of these Christian disciplines."[8]

In my book *Fresh Encounters*, I take several chapters to clarify our misconception that the "prayer closet" Jesus mentioned is primarily a private prayer chamber, pointing out that the word "closet" in Matthew 6:6 is used only in the 1611 King James Version and that all the pronouns in the model prayer are plural, not singular (*Our* Father . . . give *us* . . . *our* daily bread, etc.). The point is that leaders need to pray in community with other believers. Furthermore, the united prayer level of an organization or team never rises any higher than the personal example and passion of the senior leadership. There are many personal and organizational reasons to keep a resolute commitment to the gauge of spiritual intimacy.

Prayer-Powered Impact

I remember a number of years ago, after more than a decade of intense prayer leadership, crying out to the Lord, "How long do I have to keep up this 'prayer thing'?" In a clear way, the Lord directed my heart to a penetrating question, challenging me to endurance: "Daniel, how long will you brush your teeth, take a shower, eat breakfast, and get dressed?" I understood. It was as if the Lord said, "Why would you question the longevity of this paramount commitment any more than these other basic lifelong routines?" That settled it for me.

Since then, I resolved that the consistent pursuit of spiritual intimacy and leadership in prayer ministry is my way of life until my final day on earth. I tell leaders everywhere I go that they need to develop a vision to die on their knees. My dream, and I hope yours as well, is to seek spiritual intimacy at a personal level and lead God's people humbly into His presence until my dying day. We need to see the continuing fundamental need for prayer.

Are you convinced of the need for sincere, fervent, and ongoing prayer? Focus on the intimacy gauge—and invite others to join you, for the rest of your life.

David Peddie is the founder and president of a major commercial roofing company in Calgary, Alberta, which services clients throughout Western Canada. Several years ago, during a season of personal and professional crisis, David and his wife, Heather, were deeply touched by the power of prayer and worship, which culminated on Sunday during a visit to the Brooklyn Tabernacle. Upon returning to Calgary, their pastor asked David to describe his journey at a men's breakfast. He did, and many wept as they were convicted by the Holy Spirit of their need for personal and corporate revival. The men were convinced they needed to come together in unity and make prayer a priority in the ministry of their church.

The next week, the men started a weekly prayer meeting that soon outgrew the church. They began meeting at a local hotel. As the prayer meeting expanded, so did their vision. In Peddie's words, they asked, "What is preventing us from opening this up to the whole city?" Soon a committee was formed by Peddie to start a quarterly prayer rally. Since that time in 2003, over thirty citywide prayer rallies have occurred, attracting hundreds each time from around the Calgary area. These prayer efforts expanded, and today Peddie and a team of leaders sponsor the annual Global Day of Prayer event at the Calgary Saddledome, attracting over ten thousand people each year.

In 2007, Peddie's conviction about the power of prayer led him to hire a team of part-time intercessors to pray for his company. He notes, "It has been nothing but a sheer miracle. God has transformed our business through prayer. The intercessory prayer team prays every week throughout the building and property. Our leadership team meets with them monthly for prayer."[9]

Peddie is an example of what God can do when a businessman becomes serious about the priority of spiritual intimacy. In speaking of his routine, he notes, "I currently attend prayer meetings on Tuesday morning, Thursday morning, Wednesday night, and Sunday night. For a busy business owner, this is taking up a lot of time. But it is worth it as God is answering so many of our prayers and changing lives."

When asked why so many church and business leaders do not embrace the value of prayer, he states, "We neglect prayer because we get busy. We think we can do it on our own. We may even doubt that God answers prayer." Peddie believes that one of the keys to passionate and enduring prayer is to pray with others for regular encouragement. He offers this advice, "Don't miss. Be consistent. Invite others. Share answers to prayer. This lights a fire for prayer that continues to grow as you pray in community with others."

On the website for this prayer movement, www.calgaryprayerrally.com, one paragraph states, "Every historical revival occurred following a period of fervent prayer, fasting, and seeking the heart of God. There is a sense that Calgary is well poised to witness a revival in answer to the prayers of His people." This growing vision has emerged because God stirred one businessman to focus his heart on the gauge of spiritual intimacy, and then invite others to join him.

According to Scripture, virtually everything that truly qualifies a person for leadership is directly related to character. It's not about style, status, personal charisma, clout, or worldly measurements of success. Integrity is the main issue that makes the difference between a good leader and a bad one.

JOHN MacARTHUR
Pastor and author

So he shepherded them according to the integrity of his heart, and guided them by the skillfulness of his hands.

PSALM 78:72

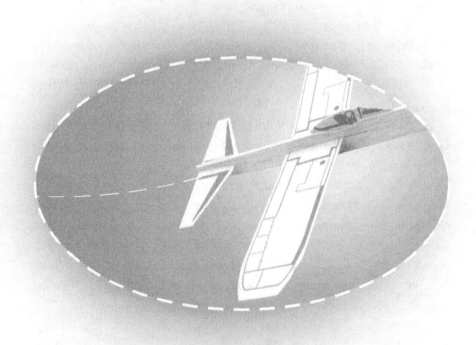

5

Gauge Three:

Personal Integrity

When people learn that on two separate occasions, in two different megachurches, I have followed a leader who experienced moral failure, they are very curious. Time and again they have asked, "How is it that a pastor can continue to lead, preach, counsel, marry, bury, and go home at night— all the while knowing he has violated his marriage covenant and disqualified himself from leadership in the church?"

Frankly, I am not sure there is a simple or standard answer. In each case, only the leader who has walked that distressing path can give an accurate response. Sometimes, even he does not know all the answers as to how and why this kind of duplicity can exist and continue over time.

In my limited assessment I typically answer with one word, "compartmentalization." The concept of compartmentalization is neutral. By definition it is the act of distributing things into classes or categories of the same type. In the fields of research, engineering, education, and biology, it is a helpful exercise. Another definition describes compartmentalization as "a mild state of dissociation."

When it comes to leadership, compartmentalization is more than a mild state of dissociation; it is usually the pathway to disaster. In this regard,

Merriam-Webster's defines it pretty accurately as "isolation or splitting off of part of the personality or mind with lack of communication and consistency between the parts."[1] I read about an illustration of this kind of behavior in the description of the popular Showtime series *Dexter*. In the series, Dexter leads a dual life as a blood splatter analyst for the local police department and is, at the same time, an altruistic serial killer. When Dexter is asked how he deals with all the gore, he responds, "I'm good at compartmentalization."[2]

Leaders who learn a pattern of compartmentalization—separating their private morality from their profession, from their relationships, from their home life, from their recreation, from their sinful secrets—have lost sight of the basic gauge of integrity.

Our English word "integrity" comes from the Latin word *integer*. Merriam-Webster's defines it as "an unimpaired condition; the quality or state of being complete or undivided."[3] Integrity is the opposite of compartmentalization. It is a life where all the pieces fit together in a wholesome and spiritually authentic way.

A King Learns about Integrity

As we return to the leadership instrument panel to consider the gauge of integrity, we focus on one Bible passage, a psalm written by David, a man after God's own heart (Acts 13:22). Psalm 15 reveals a moment when the king resolved to embrace the meaning of real integrity at a deeper level than ever before.

At the time, David wrestled with his own storm. Reputable scholars believe he penned this psalm while in exile, after a painful political coup led by his embittered son Absalom (2 Samuel 15–17).[4] In those days, heartbroken over an estranged son and hurting over the betrayal of many loyal subjects, the king was far from his palace in Jerusalem. Now he prepared for attack by Absalom and the entire army of Israel. Every aspect of his future and even his very life lay in heart-wrenching uncertainty.

In the midst of this incredible turmoil, he penned these words:

Lord, who may abide in Your tabernacle? Who may dwell in Your holy hill?

He who walks uprightly, and works righteousness, and speaks the truth in his heart; he who does not backbite with his tongue, nor does evil to his neighbor, nor does he take up a reproach against his friend; in whose eyes a vile person is despised, but he honors those who fear the Lord; he who swears to his own hurt and does not change; he who does not put out his money at usury, nor does he take a bribe against the innocent.

He who does these things shall never be moved. (Psalm 15)

This passage has become the paramount picture of integrity for my own life. It is a clear portrayal of the integrity gauge, especially in times of leadership crisis and confusion.

As he wrote, David pondered the marks of the spiritually authentic God-follower. The Spirit inspired a practical list of the marks of a leader who will "never be moved" (Psalm 15:5b). Psalm 15 neatly breaks down into descriptions of personal integrity, interpersonal integrity, and financial integrity.

The Right Question

David begins with a question. It is not a superficial inquiry about the circumstances or personalities of the present situation nor even about the future outcome. This question deals with matters of the heart, which is always the right initial focus during personal crisis.

In asking, "Lord, who may abide in Your tabernacle? Who may dwell in Your holy hill?" David wants to understand the character of the person who is spiritually authentic and thus will truly know the presence and blessing of Yahweh. As he writes these words, he is in the wilderness, unable to worship at Zion. Absalom and his loyal subjects are in charge, going through the motions of worship. It is truly a moment of spiritual crisis and confusion.

David is asking for a reiteration of the elements of the life that God will bless and protect. He is looking for God's definition, not the current public assessment of who is right and wrong.

Personal Integrity

Inspired by God's Spirit, David begins to define the marks of a life of genuine integrity. Throughout this psalm, David receives divine wisdom and specificity for his own heart—and for our hearts as we read his relevant descriptions of a blameless life.

The first words on the parchment provide a powerful definition of personal integrity: "He who walks uprightly, and works righteousness, and speaks the truth in his heart" (v. 2). Notice the outward to inward flow. Outwardly, he is upright or blameless; he "walks with integrity" (NASB). Again, this is a lifestyle where the pieces fit together and there is no apparent breach of honor or holy living that would bring blame against his life.

Moving inward, the psalm explains that an upright life is composed of righteous works. This is the person who always seeks to do the right thing. Of course, we know that the only ultimate way this can occur is through the power of a new nature and righteous heart made possible by the grace of Jesus Christ (2 Corinthians 5:21).

At the core of this life is a love for truth that results in self-honesty. It says he "speaks the truth in his heart" (v. 2). This inner reality is also reflected in David's great confessional prayer in Psalm 51, where he writes, "Behold, You desire truth in the inward parts, and in the hidden part You will make me to know wisdom" (51:6). After months of covering up his sin with Bathsheba and the murder of her husband, Uriah, David came to understand the power and freedom of an honest heart before God.

Personal integrity, then, begins with truth at the core of our being. This produces right living, which comprises a lifestyle of integrity. In the vortex of his profound and complex crisis, David is inspired to come back to issues of the heart with such clarity and precision.

Interpersonal Integrity

Most of the Psalms deal with relationships. No doubt, a lot of relationships had gone bad, which fueled the current crisis. David's relationship with Absalom had been strained for years. Absalom "stole the hearts of the men of Israel" (2 Samuel 15:6). The whole situation was marked by lies, betrayal, double crossing, anger, and mistrust. A dose of definition was desperately needed if David was going to embrace integrity in the midst of the chaos.

Five aspects of relational integrity appear in verses 3–4. First, integrity is evidenced in *what we say about others*. God's answer to David's question begins with this important truth, "He who does not backbite with his tongue." This is the idea of someone who "walks along" with slander or gossip on his lips. It is the old idea of a "talebearer." This person inflicts harm on others through unkind, unnecessary, and often untrue statements—usually flowing from a heart that is filled with untruth. The New Testament equivalent is the word *diabolos*, which is also a name for "the Devil" and gives strong indication of the nature and evil of a backbiting tongue.

Second, relational integrity is evidenced in *what we do to others*. Verse 3b reads, "Nor does evil to his neighbor." Romans 12:17 is the best commentary on this idea: "Repay no one evil for evil. Have regard for good things in the sight of all men." After a discussion about those who are at enmity with us, verse 21 reiterates "Do not be overcome by evil, but overcome evil with good."

Bitterness, revenge, and payback are tempting reactions in the midst of a leadership storm. I can only imagine the emotions David must have battled in this arena, given all the betrayal and pain. God reminds David, and us, that having good intentions is the right response to bad situations that have delivered a dose of hurt and disloyalty to our lives. Beware; even the best leaders can hit a sudden and deadly tailspin when they allow bitterness and quiet revenge to take root in their hearts.

Verse 3c adds, "Nor does he take up a reproach against his friend." This tells us that integrity is also an issue of *what I receive about others*. It's been said, "You may be lord of your tongue, but I am also master of my ears." In our modern-day free-for-all of information and juicy tidbits about almost anyone, we are still responsible for what we hear and embrace. Integrity refuses to give attention to the latest blather about people and refuses to believe anything negative about another person unless the evidence of multiple witnesses confirms it. In David's situation, much had been said and heard by the disloyal Israelites. God fixes David's attention, not on others, but on his own gauge of integrity and how he will respond to the latest "word on the street."

- -

Five Marks of Interpersonal Integrity

Interpersonal integrity, sometimes known as relational integrity, reveals our attitudes and behavior toward people we meet throughout our lives. Here are five marks of healthy interpersonal integrity:

1. Healthy speech. When we are away from a person, we speak well of the individual. There is no slander or gossip.
2. Good deeds. We display good behavior to individuals, even when their actions show indifference or hostility toward us. Instead of feeling bitter or wanting to pay back a perceived (or even real) injustice, we show them respect and treat them with kind deeds.
3. Attuned ears. We are selective in what we listen to about others. If someone would complain or gossip about another, we refuse to believe anything negative about the person (unless the evidence of multiple witnesses confirms it).
4. Proper evaluation. We ignore people's evaluations of those we know and seek to understand God's right evaluation, thus honoring those who honor God, even if they can do nothing for us or are not popular.
5. Reliable words. People can count on our word as being reliable; our statements reflect a commitment to the truth (see Matthew 5:37).

- -

Fourth, the passage links integrity to *how I associate with others*. The text reads, "In whose eyes a vile person is despised, but he honors those who fear the Lord" (v. 4a). Too many times, we compromise integrity in whom we honor, elevate, and pay attention to—based on their personal popularity, financial status, or influence in a given situation. David learns that integrity "calls it as it is," based on God's assessment, not man's. A person of real integrity works hard at bestowing honor on people simply because they fear the Lord, regardless of whether or not they can do anything for us. In our scramble to network, climb the ladder, acquire endorsements, and connect with the latest and coolest, we can walk very close to the edge of compromise in this regard.

Verse 4 also carries a warning for every believer, especially leaders, about the kind of entertainment we digest and delight in. "Honor" involves the allocation of our time, our attention, our words, and our money. Too many believers guzzle down whatever is being dished out in the latest Hollywood feeding fest, without the discernment this verse demands. This pattern in our lives can begin to redefine our values if we are not careful. In that slow redefinition, integrity is lost and the leadership flight veers off course.

The fifth aspect of real interpersonal integrity deals with the reliability of our words. Verse 4c says, "He who swears to his own hurt and does not change." This is the issue of *what we commit to others*. Obviously, Jesus nailed this issue when He spoke to the incredulous Pharisees of His day, "But let your 'Yes' be 'Yes' and your 'No,' 'No.' For whatever is more than these is from the evil one" (Matthew 5:37). The apostle James also warns against superficial "swearing" lest we "fall into judgment" (5:12). This is strong medicine when it says that an inability to keep one's word is the work of the Evil One and brings judgment upon a person. But, by God's definition of integrity, a leader must say what he means and mean what he says— even if fidelity to one's word inflicts pain or loss.

In a world of unprecedented compromise, where the rules of a situation change based on convenience or personal gain, this definition of integrity shouts with relevance. Again, David's current mess had been intensified by broken promises and redefined loyalties. God issues a clear word about credible words.

Financial Integrity

In our "show me the money" culture, this final clarification of the integrity gauge is essential. The text says, "He who does not put out his money at usury, nor does he take a bribe against the innocent" (v. 5). Charging interest was not a problem when Israel was dealing with other nations, but it was greedy and hurtful when interacting with a fellow Israelite (Deuteronomy 23:19–20). The only time a fellow Israelite needed to borrow in those days was during a situation of destitution, when he lacked basic food, clothing, or housing. Integrity demands a generous and giving heart that is motivated to help and bless others in need. Charging monetary interest would poison the heart and the relationships because it involved greed and a willingness to hurt someone else, just to make another buck.

Equally lacking in integrity was the person who would accept a bribe. While charging interest involves the outflow of personal funds, bribery is connected to the inflow of money. In all likelihood, Israel's current crisis had been fueled by various forms of bribery. To do something hurtful toward others because of "what is in it for me" is wrong and signals a breach of integrity.

The Promise

The leader who watches the integrity gauge finds blessings: "he shall not be moved." The situation was looking pretty bleak for David as the entire army of Israel, under Absalom's embittered leadership, was coming after his head. Yet, he embraced the Spirit's promise: "He who does these things shall never be moved."

Obviously, the promise does not imply a problem-free life. This is literally the assurance that we will never be overcome by insecurity, fear, or internal self-destruction. Psalm 15–type intimacy with God and related integrity produces well-being and hope, in spite of the circumstances. This is the same assurance Jesus promised, "Anyone who listens to my teaching and obeys me is wise, like a person who builds a house on solid rock. Though the rain comes in torrents and the floodwaters rise and the winds beat against that house, it won't collapse because it is built on bedrock" (Matthew 7:24–25 NLT).

A Psalm 15 Leadership Approach

In 1983 David Frauenshuh started a commercial real estate company specializing in developing medical facilities. He began with four employees. Today Frauenshuh, Inc. employs 120 workers and is among the top five largest medical developers in the United States, doing business in twenty-two states. At any given time the company manages about five million square feet of properties.

David and his wife, Sandra, are known for their vibrant faith. Even though he is a very busy executive, his values motivate him to spend 40 percent of his time on faith issues in the community. He serves on the national board of the Salvation Army (and other ministry boards), provides significant leadership in community prayer events, shares his testimony in many civic settings, and takes time to disciple younger believers both in his church and in the network of his business activities.

Recently, I sat down with David at his corporate headquarters. I asked the question, "If you had a group of young businessmen sitting around the table and could give them just one leadership principle that you value above all else, what would it be?"

Frauenshuh's response was immediate and instinctive. He quoted the unofficial company motto, "Integrity above all else." Then he amplified: "It's all about integrity. Leadership starts with integrity. It is about the way you manage your life, your people, and your customers." The parallel of Frauenshuh's answers with the principles of Psalm 15 are uncanny, although intentional.

A person's life is the core of who he is when he's alone or with family and the friends who know him best. Frauenshuh noted that your behavior then extends to larger circles of your coworkers and employees; these are the real tests of how you relate with grace and truth. Finally, how you treat customers as you make money will reflect your true integrity. "If you do not operate in an upright way, customers can smell it a mile away."

Consistent with the powerful Psalm 15 promise of security, Frauenshuh noted, "When you have integrity in these three areas, there is such ease with life. You don't have to second-guess or cover up. You don't have any worries. If you are cheating on your wife, you're mistreating employees, you're not honest with customers—you are very confused, and will become very insecure."

David and I agreed that keeping integrity is hard work, but violating it is even harder work. A leader who has lost sight of the integrity gauge will spend enormous amounts of energy trying to cover up character breaches rather than living with confidence and authentic hope.

Quoting his mother's wisdom, Frauenshuh said simply, "Don't make problems for yourself." Indeed, the very nature of leadership is filled with enough problems. The wisdom stands: Don't make problems for yourself. Display integrity in all your dealings; then your gauge called personal integrity will help you to defy gravity when storms come.

*I'm always described as "cocksure" or "with a swagger,"
and that bears no resemblance to who I feel like inside.
I feel plagued by insecurity.*

BEN AFFLECK
Actor

*. . . and have put on the new man who is
renewed in knowledge according to the
image of Him who created him.*

COLOSSIANS 3:10

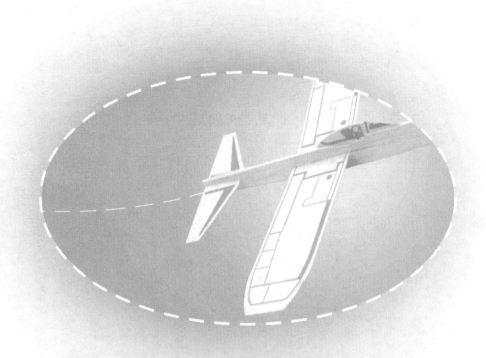

6

Gauge Four:

Biblical Identity

I sat in the living room across from a handsome, intelligent, and well-spoken young man in his late twenties. He was the son of a renowned pastor who cheated on his wife, this young man's mother. As we discussed the situation and the choices his parents faced, I asked what he thought they would do. I will never forget his reply, "Mom won't leave Dad because her whole identity is wrapped up in being a pastor's wife. And Dad will eventually get back into the ministry because it's who he is. It is all he knows. Right or wrong, that is just the way it is with them."

This fallen pastor did eventually get back into ministry, stumbling again and compounding the hurt and disgrace that had already taken a colossal toll on many lives.

When a leader's identity is rooted in superficial roles, responsibilities, ambitions, and achievements, he is vulnerable to a kind of emotional and relational vertigo that results in disaster. A misguided sense of identity is the elemental ingredient of personal insecurity. Insecure leaders are unhealthy to the core of who they are. They build dysfunctional organizations and usually finish the leadership flight with an empty heart and damaged followers.

When it comes to our identity, we can spend our lives (1) searching for our identity, (2) trying to prove our identity, or (3) confidently living out our identity.[1] The third option is, by far, the preferred option. Our identity should rest securely on the unchanging truth of who we are in Christ.

An Unchanging Identity

As leaders we can easily fall into the trap of basing our identity on things that can suddenly change. Our job or work title can change. Our feelings of success or effective performance can be subjective and fleeting. Our financial status can be downgraded quickly. Our physical appearance eventually will deteriorate. (It's called aging.) Even the roles and relationships we fulfill can be dramatically impacted by crisis. One day I may be a father. The next day I may lose my child (or children, as Job did). I may be married one year and widowed or divorced the next.

This issue of changing roles and relationships is very personal to me as I write. Although I still lead the prayer effort at a megachurch as a part-time pastor, my title, position, and influence have changed dramatically. I am now on the road as a "spiritual pyromaniac" about forty times a year, helping people rekindle their spiritual life. When I followed this calling, I left a substantial senior pastor suite on the top floor of a 350,000-square-foot building, overlooking a meadow and a pond. For the next eighteen months, I had no office. My treasured and sizable library remained in boxes collecting dust. I was really a ministry gypsy. That will test your identity.

As a senior pastor, I had known the relative security of the pastoral role with the ability to take offerings each Sunday and appeal to the congregation when we had a financial need. Now I am really a missionary with a parachurch paradigm. I live on monthly support from a circle of committed friends and honoraria. Prayer and revival is not an easy arena to capture hearts for fund-raising purposes. As of this writing, the American economy is more unstable than it's been in decades. My identity would be very fragile right now if it rested on financial security. I remind my heart regularly that net worth is not the same as self-worth.

My wife and I are now watching our children leave the nest in rapid-fire fashion. All three have left home in pursuit of their dreams in a matter of one year. My identity as a dad has changed. Our roles as parents are totally new and different.

Again, identity cannot be based in things that change—and almost everything in this life does change, like it or not. Leaders must keep their eye on the gauge of *biblical identity* throughout their flight, an instrument that acts as a stabilizing influence in our life. The unsettling dynamics of gains and losses in this life can get our eyes off the truth and onto the emotions and struggles of the moment. This can create a deep insecurity that hinders effective leadership.

A *Wall Street Journal* article suggests that people of low self-esteem can manage but can never lead. Capturing the need for leaders who are secure, the article states: "If you want to manage somebody, manage yourself. Do that well and you'll be ready to stop managing and start leading."[2]

Research psychologist Abraham Maslow concluded that persons of low self-esteem are not only more frenzied in their lifestyles, but are also less imaginative. As a result they are far less likely to become successful leaders than persons who have better learned to manage the insecure inner foe of self.[3]

Christ-Esteem as Self-Esteem

Larry Crabb, a well-known Christian counselor and author, is noted for saying that a healthy self-image is seeing yourself as God sees you, no more, no less. Effective and enduring leadership is the expression of a healthy self-image, not the search for one. New life in Christ changes everything, especially how we see ourselves, thus affecting how we lead.

Paul Hontz has served as the senior pastor of Central Wesleyan Church in Holland, Michigan, since 1977. Today, Central is one of the largest Wesleyan churches in the United States with a multifaceted ministry to their community and around the globe. He has learned to find his esteem in Christ, but at first he struggled to put his identity fully in Him. In his forthright style, Paul tells the story of how insecurity almost threatened to undermine his ministry.

Journey to Security

His own journey from insecurity to a deep sense of emotional health started with a phone call he received from an anonymous person who did not attend his church but had just overheard a conversation in a restaurant between two staff members from Central. The conversation was very derogatory toward Hontz. This person was concerned and wanted the senior pastor to be aware.

As it turned out, one of these staff members was the previous pastor, who still served on staff (an early indicator of trouble). When Hontz inquired, the two men were apologetic for the public revelation of their sentiments, but they were very open and aggressive about their accusations toward Hontz and his leadership. This created an ongoing tempest that took some time to resolve.

Through the process of this first major leadership crisis, Hontz began to see some deep insecurities that kept him from openly confronting the problems of the ministry. Instead, he tended to bottle his emotions deep inside in the name of "humility and meekness." In his own words, "Because of my insecurities I would just hold it all inside and this created incredible turmoil. It got to the point where I had to swallow my pride and go see a counselor."[4]

Eventually, Pastor Hontz began to realize that real security in Christ would allow him to understand and be honest about his emotions. He learned that he could have the strength to embrace his identity in Christ in such a way that he could practice "honest Christian assertiveness" as opposed to an "unchristian" passivity or aggression, both of which are often expressions of insecurity. Hontz speaks of being freed up to accept responsibility for what he was feeling and to manage it from a perspective of security rather than insecurity.

Hontz advises, "Until a young leader gets to the point where he is confident in his identity in Christ, he will struggle to say 'no' to others or ask others for help without feeling guilty. This kind of insecurity can be devastating personally, to your family, and to those who follow you. And, this issue has huge ramifications for your own satisfaction and personal fulfillment. It will impact the life of your children and your marriage—and certainly the life of the church. An inaccurate sense of identity and spirituality will eventually damage your children and taint your ministry."

How to Have a Vital Biblical Identity

So how do we move beyond an inaccurate sense of identity and spirituality to become secure and healthy? How do we lead people from a position of security rather than insecurity? Here are three factors that can lead to a reliable identity gauge.

1. Embrace the Truth

I've said hundreds of times over the years that "the hardest thing about the Christian life is that it is so *daily*." We know that every day we must experience renewal in the inner man (2 Corinthians 4:16). We also know that we must be transformed by the renewing of our minds, rather than conforming to the messages and approaches of this world (Romans 12:2). We know that we are new creatures in Christ (2 Corinthians 5:17). So every day, the quest for security is won by a focused affirmation of the truth about our true identity as Christians and leaders. This may seem elementary, but it is, in fact, one of the primary commitments of excellent leadership.

Consider this command: "Put on the new self, which in the likeness of God has been created in righteousness and holiness of the truth" (Ephesians 4:24 NASB). Colossians 3:10 underscores this same truth when it says we have "put on the new man who is renewed in knowledge according to the image of Him who created him." Personally, I find this truth incredibly practical and liberating.

So, as a Christ-follower—and as a leader—take the time to regularly study the truth of who you are in Christ. Many writers have presented this idea in various books[5]—but the power is in making it real to your own leadership through a proactive study and affirmation. For me, it comes down to a personal identity statement that I have written and memorized, and that I review every day. I even have it on my iPod, as part of a daily renewal system I have developed.[6] Every day I remind myself: "I, Daniel D. Henderson, am a new creature in Jesus Christ—a completely loved, fully accepted, and totally empowered child of the most loving, most high, most holy God. I have been created by His amazing grace for a life full of good works and God's glory through Christ, my Lord."

You could certainly craft such a statement, and probably with much better words and flow. This one works for me daily; it keeps me in flight, because it is the truth of who I am as I live and lead through the unpredictable and unsettling storms of life.

Alfred Adler, the Austrian psychiatrist whose influential system of individual psychology introduced the term "inferiority feeling" (later widely and often inaccurately called "inferiority complex"), described the personal battle in these words, "Imperfect preparation gives rise to the thousand-fold forms that express physical and mental inferiority and insecurity."

The great "preparation" for overcoming insecurity and confidently living out our true identity is a commitment to daily renew in the truth of who we really are in Christ.

2. Expose the Lies

Leaders must regularly expose the "identity lies" for what they are. Those lies are formed based on subjective and superficial input. Sometimes we can keep believing the early, negative life-messages from parents or even the "nicknames" of our childhood. Difficult experiences in our past can make us feel unworthy, or "dirty," or inferior. External comparisons can tank our perspective as we get caught up in contrasting our status, appearance, or achievements with others. Such comparisons eventually can significantly undermine the well-being and positive impact of a leader.

Again, a key to leadership is making wise choices about what we believe. We must recognize that self-perceptions or feelings of inferiority are not the ultimate reality. We must reject them in exchange for the truth of what God says about us based on the complete and sufficient work of Christ.

Identity Lies

Society and Satan each can plant lies into our minds about who we are as people of God. Here are some of those lies you can replace with biblical truth:

1. "I am a failure." Jesus of Nazareth seemed a failure to the disciples and family members while on the cross, but He was elevated for seeking the right thing—honor for the Father and sacrificial love for others (Philippians 2:7–9).
2. I'm not as accomplished, handsome, popular as . . . This is the lie of comparison—that we must achieve or be more than others to have worth. There will always be someone who will surpass us, just as someone will always have more wealth than you or I. Comparison is a vain, endless path we need not walk.
3. "I'm not worthy of God's forgiveness for this failure." But Jesus died for unworthy sinners, not for worthy ones (Romans 5:8), so His forgiveness is available to all.

---

3. Express the Reality

A leader's example of living in the reality of his true identity will reassure and inspire followers.

Back in the early 1980s, Ken Campbell was a dental student in the Chicago area. He and his fiancée were stopped at a light on an exit ramp next to a tanker truck filled with gasoline. An eighteen-wheel tractor trailer exiting the ramp experienced brake failure and slammed into the back of the tanker next to Ken's car. The Campbell vehicle immediately was engulfed in flames. Ken's fiancée died in the crash; he suffered severe, life-threatening burns over most of his body.

His very life was "touch and go" for weeks. The pain and heartbreak were unbearable. After months of excruciating treatments, multiple skin grafts, cosmetic surgeries, and ongoing therapy to improve his blood circulation, Ken started life over again. On the outside, he looked completely different. To some his appearance was probably difficult to view. But on the inside, Ken Campbell was still Ken Campbell—only stronger and better. His love for God's Word had grown.

As part of a leadership class that Ken attended when I was his pastor, he memorized the entire book of 2 Timothy. He loved the hopeful theme of 2 Timothy 1:12: "For this reason I also suffer these things; nevertheless I am not ashamed, for I know whom I have believed and am persuaded that He is able to keep what I have committed to Him until that Day."

Ken embraced the resolve of 4:5, "But you be watchful in all things, endure afflictions, do the work of an evangelist, fulfill your ministry."

Thanks to the power of God's Word and the enduring love of family and friends, Ken is more in touch with himself and his Lord than ever. His love for God's truth helped him embrace his identity and calling in a way that turned his tragedy into triumph.

After all the medical attention, the popular ABC-TV program *The Wide World of Sports* featured Ken's story. Ken had recovered and become an avid runner, and ABC spotlighted him during an iron man triathlon competition, as Ken swam, biked, and ran in Hawaii. More recently, he took an early retirement from a successful dental practice in Sacramento. He is also a respected leader in local politics and an avid student of God's Word. Ken is a model because he has learned that *Ken is not his skin.*

Like Ken, every leader must accept the pain and struggle of the difficult storms of this life. Then we must anchor our soul in the truth of what God tells us about our true self. With that reliable anchor, we can lead, love, and live in consistent victory and security.

Journey to Freedom

Dave Gudgel, senior pastor of Bethany Bible Church in Phoenix, has watched his congregation become a vibrant church again, as it was in the early days, when it planted daughter churches that became lights for the gospel throughout the metropolitan area. But his early years in the pastorate did not seem so rewarding. In his first senior pastorate, he felt "frustrated and discouraged by the lack of numerical results. The growth wasn't happening like I had anticipated, hoped, or dreamed.

"I felt like a failure," he admitted. "God used this time to purify my motives and teach me where He wanted my focus."[7]

That was when Pastor Dave began to recognize the truth and expose the lies. Through a journey of focused study and deep renewal, Dave began to find a new freedom from the "*Success Syndrome.*" He anchored his soul in the truth that God had called him to be faithful, not successful. As he says, "That one thought alone continues to liberate my life and ministry from a performance-based ministry." He exposed the lie that his identity lay in personal success.

In summarizing his journey, Pastor Gudgel notes, "When our identity is based on anything else but Christ, we can easily end up thinking too much or too little of ourselves. Either way, we become someone other than the person the Lord has called us to be. When we look to Christ for our identity, we will not compare ourselves with others, nor put ourselves down, nor look to others for our sense of worth or value."

*I hope when I die there will be at least five of
my friends who will be able to sit through
my funeral without looking at their watches.*

THE LEADER OF A LARGE CHRISTIAN ORGANIZATION
talking with R. C. Sproul

*A man who isolates himself seeks his own desire;
he rages against all wise judgment.*

PROVERBS 18:1

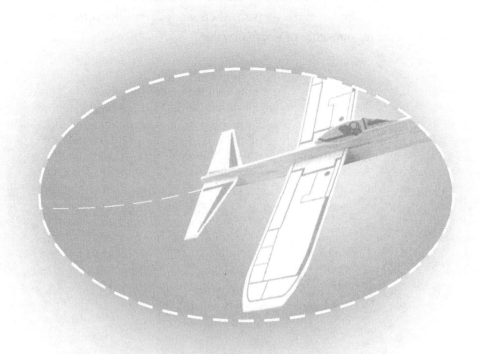

7

Gauge Five:

Genuine Accountability

Consider an existence where you have never seen a reflection of your physical appearance. Take away even the possibility of seeing your image in a window or the waters of a quiet pond. Imagine a world without mirrors.

Go a step further and imagine a world without portraits, photographs, or videos. You have no idea what your face, hair, or body look like from the perspective of other people.

Taking the scenario even further, imagine that all the other people in the world have duct tape over their mouths. They cannot begin to describe your physical appearance to you. You do not know if your nose is big, small, or average; the color of your eyes remains a mystery. You might be very handsome or beautiful. You might be very ugly. You can never know.

Try as we may, it is almost impossible to imagine what this would be like in our actual world—one full of mirrors, photos, and abundant input from others eager to give us their opinion about the way we look. Obviously, I've just described a very limited and subjective existence. Yet this is an apt illustration of the emotional, spiritual, and social reality of a leader who does not understand and embrace the incredible value of genuine accountability.

Genuine accountability is a mirror to the soul, providing vital feedback for many aspects of a life well lived. Accountability fuels proper perspective and encourages authentic purity. In contrast, one of the common ingredients in every leadership crash is isolation and subjectivity.

The Right Kind of Mirrors

If you have ever stopped to view yourself at one of those rows of mirrors at the state fair or local carnival, you know that not all mirrors provide an accurate reflection. Some make you look quite distorted, with a bubble in the middle, stub legs, or a head twice the normal size. Others stretch you out, thin and long, the victim of a diet gone awry. And if you have ever walked through one of those "house of mirrors" at the carnival, you realize too many mirrors can create confusion.

Real accountability is more than simply having mirrors. It is having the right kind of mirrors, coupled with an intentional and consistent determination to use them for frank assessment and input that forces us to speak truth and grow in our character. Real accountability thrives in an environment of humility and transparency for the sake of character development and ultimate service to Christ and others.

Accountability is more than surrounding yourself with other people. It is more than having a circle of friends or a few golfing buddies. It is more than simply getting input from others. It's having true friends who give a genuine, candid reflection of the true you.

During a recent news interview, Pennsylvania Governor Ed Rendell discussed the scandal involving then–Illinois Governor Rod Blagojevich, who was arrested on federal corruption charges after allegedly trying to "sell" an Illinois senate seat vacated by president–elect Barack Obama to the highest bidder. The television host asked Rendell how politicians get to the point of behaving in a risky and unethical fashion. Rendell's response was candid and insightful. "They surround themselves with 'yes men,' and based on the input of these advisors, they believe they can do no wrong—that they are invincible."

Some believe former Governor Blagojevich had some mirrors that were neither accurate nor truthful. The consequences of this lack of real accountability proved to be appalling.

Concerning this lack of real accountability, author Ken Blanchard writes, "Too often in an organization, self-serving leaders cut off feedback by killing the messenger. Eventually the anti feedback leader gets blindsided even though people were available who could have given helpful information." He goes on to say, "Bring truth-tellers into your life, and they'll be there if they know that you'll listen. It doesn't mean you have to do everything that they say, but they want to be heard. And in the process if you'll share some of your vulnerability, then that give and take is fabulous."[1]

Leaders cannot afford to believe the lie that genuine friends are a luxury. They cannot believe that Lone Ranger leadership is acceptable or healthy. They cannot afford to surround themselves with people who will only tell them the easy and positive things. We all have blind spots that can become gaping holes in the fuselage of our leadership if we are not receiving feedback from people outside our subjective struggles who will tell us the truth. Paul wrote to the Galatians, "Have I therefore become your enemy because I tell you the truth?" (4:16). Leaders cannot afford to let any of the truth-tellers in their lives feel this way.

The Core of Divine Accountability

True accountability is found inside the individual. Pastor and author John MacArthur notes, "If you don't win the battle on the inside, all the human accountability can be manipulated. You can say as much or as little as you want to say to anyone. You can play games with most people."

MacArthur adds, "My greatest accountability lies with the Lord; to love the Lord with all my heart, soul, mind, and strength. This is where my highest accountability lies—with the only one who cannot be deceived. Leaders need to realize that time and truth go hand in hand. Given enough time, the truth will come out."[2]

The apostle James uses the mirror analogy to describe a life that receives the objective input of God's truth to the soul (1:22–25). The apostle warns us not to glance in the mirror and quickly forget what we have seen.

Instead, we are to gaze into God's truth, described as the "law of liberty." This gaze creates an authentic life of applied truth and results in great blessing. A failure to engage in this gaze creates lifestyle vertigo, marked by self-deception.

Using his own mirror metaphor, Paul tells us that we all are beholding as in a mirror the glory of the Lord and are being transformed into Christ's image as the Spirit works within us (2 Corinthians 3:18). This intimate accountability—looking toward Jesus and being honest before Him—is the beginning place of an authentic life. In fact, in the very next chapter of 2 Corinthians, Paul describes his own testimony of this accountability to the Lord, showing how such accountability to the Lord has resulted in a life without any "hidden shame" and a ministry that manifests truth, shining forth the light of an intimate walk with Christ (see 2 Corinthians 4:2–6). This is a life that truly soars.

The Circle of Interpersonal Accountability

Hebrews 3:12–15 reminds us of the power of divine accountability, coupled with the essential input from other truth-tellers. "Beware, brethren, lest there be in any of you an evil heart of unbelief in departing from the living God; but exhort one another daily, while it is called 'Today,' lest any of you be hardened through the deceitfulness of sin. For we have become partakers of Christ if we hold the beginning of our confidence steadfast to the end, while it is said: 'Today, if you will hear His voice, do not harden your hearts as in the rebellion.'"

Clearly we need the daily exhortation of fellow believers, family members, and courageous and godly associates as a means of preventing a hard heart and pattern of self-deception. The Bible gives us many illustrations of this kind of healthy input. Moses' father-in-law, Jethro, was able to see things that Moses was blind to as the leader labored under extreme overload. Jethro's honest and wise input alleviated Moses' burdens and allowed a leadership team to emerge for the good of the people (Exodus 18:13–17). Centuries later David was helped by the courageous and objective input of Jonathan, whose warnings about King Saul, Jonathan's father, saved David's life when he was being hunted by Saul (1 Samuel 20). Later, David was jolted to repentance and restoration by the strong confrontation of the prophet Nathan who was willing to tell him of his hurtful sin (2 Samuel 12:1–13).

Paul confronted Peter when Peter's fear of man manifested in hypocrisy and doublespeak (Galatians 2:11–16). Likewise, Paul's objective observation about the way fear was paralyzing Timothy's ministry effectiveness helped Paul's protégé (2 Timothy 1:7–8).

Leaders are commanded to confront and even publicly expose fellow elders who persist in self-destructive behavior. This kind of accountability is healthy for the entire church as it instills a genuine fear of the detrimental results of sin (1 Timothy 5:20).

Luis Bush helped originate the term "10/40 Window" to describe the region of the world between the tenth and fortieth latitudes with the greatest human suffering and least exposure to the gospel. Though he has served as the international director of the AD2000 & Beyond Movement (1989–2001) and currently leads Transform World, a global effort to bring leaders together for prayer and strategic outreach, he recognizes his need for accountability. Because we live in the same town, we have become accountability partners and close friends; we meet regularly for accountability in our walk with the Lord and our marriages.

Luis first discovered the power of accountability in 1986 while serving as CEO of Partners International, a missions agency that supports indigenous missionaries in nations around the world. Luis felt completely overwhelmed by the demands and complexity of his assignment. But he was willing to begin a time of honest self-disclosure and vulnerability, establishing an ongoing accountability that has helped Luis in profound ways over the years, keeping him on course during his leadership flights.

"I turned to a trusted friend, Milan Telian, who on one of our first meetings asked me to write a list of my weaknesses and strengths and he would do the same," Luis wrote. "When we shared these on the second week, he suggested I go back and work a little more on my weaknesses as the list was somewhat short. That vulnerability was the beginning of a trusted friendship that not only served well during the crisis time where Milan stepped up to provide needed support and accountability to help me gain spiritual 'altitude' and perspective at Partners International, but it has lasted more than twenty years. Around that core relationship of vulnerability and openness with Milan was built an accountability group of five godly men in different vocations that has made so much difference to me and my wife—and which is still active and functional today, after two decades."[3]

In discussing an accountability commitment, Luis said, "A healthy, consistent accountability gives permission to anyone in the group to initiate the conversation, ask for a conference call, and ask the tough questions. There is no topic that is out of bounds. The scope of accountability is personal, family, and ministry. Many times I have been helped to make better decisions. Of course, the danger is that an accountability group can become indifferent, inconsistent, or overbearing. In my case, it has been a great source of strength and wisdom."

Seeking Accountability in Crisis

Such accountability benefits all leaders, not just those speaking from the pulpit. Paul Molitor played Major League Baseball (MLB) for twenty-one seasons with the Milwaukee Brewers, Toronto Blue Jays, and Minnesota Twins. With a lifetime batting average of .306 and more than 3,300 hits during his career, Molitor was elected to the Hall of Fame in 2004, his first year of eligibility. Paul served as a team leader in MLB and for several years also coordinated his team's baseball chapel. Today he loves Christ and is actively involved in a ministry to men around the nation, calling them to accountability, especially in the area of sexual purity.

There was a time, however, when Molitor was caught in leadership vertigo. After some bad decisions that threatened his spiritual health, his marriage, and his family—Paul recognized that he was hiding, and living in dishonesty toward family and friends.

Greg Grow, a pastor from previous days, welcomed Molitor's call on a day when Paul realized his desperate need for help. Greg's friendship became a source of personal survival. Greg accepted Paul in his brokenness and was committed to honest and unwavering input. He pointed Paul to the truth of God's Word, guiding him beyond head knowledge to an

---

A Sevenfold Commitment

One group of men have learned to be accountable to each other through a sevenfold commitment that reflects covenantal relationship among the men:

1. A covenant of love: An unconditional commitment to the good of the other men
2. A covenant of prayer: A resolve to pray regularly and consistently with and for one another
3. A covenant of availability: A commitment to "2 a.m. Friendships" that are willing to respond at any time no matter the sacrifice
4. A covenant of accountability: A determination to pursue and persevere in regular connections with one another
5. A covenant of honesty: A willingness to tell the truth and not hide failures and needs from one another
6. A covenant of vulnerability: A submission to the truth of the Word and the Spirit who flows into interpersonal relationships
7. A covenant of confidentiality: A sacred trust to protect one another and the information shared[4]

---

authentic application of principles of forgiveness, restoration, spiritual authenticity, and integrity.

In addition to his ongoing consistent accountability with Pastor Grow, Molitor has developed strong covenantal relationships with another small group of brothers. Under the guidance of one of his pastors, he has embraced a sevenfold commitment with these men, shown in the sidebar, "A Sevenfold Commitment."

Molitor says of the commitment among the men, "It is not something you can expect to come from eight or nine people. You will be fortunate to find one, maybe a couple. You just have to be committed to find that person in your life can meet that covenantal [criteria]. It is easy to be friends to many, but a leader must be diligent to make accountability a part of his leadership development."[5]

The Broader Circle of Multifaceted Accountability

Sid Verdoorn served as president of The C. H. Robinson Company for twenty-five years. During his tenure he led the company to astounding growth and success. One secret to his effectiveness is what he describes as a "culture of accountability."

Verdoorn's sense of accountability came from his roots in a small Minnesota town where his early family models were people of outstanding honesty. Likewise, the small-town culture created strong awareness of one another's lives and well-being. This carried over into Sid's business leadership; he created a strong sense of accountability within the staff with clear standards of behavior and strong consequences for violating those principles. Verdoorn promoted employee accountability to their constituency as well. "We are accountable to every customer all around the world to live by our core values, and it must start with how we function as a team," he told me. "As a leader, I never allowed layers of bureaucracy. We are all accountable to one another and everyone we serve. With seven thousand employees worldwide, each with family members and needs, accountability was essential. That's a lot of responsibility."[6]

In thinking of the accountability of his life, Pastor John MacArthur states, "My accountability is endless. I am accountable to every person who has ever heard me preach a sermon, listened to a CD, or read a page in a book that I have written." For John, that involves millions of people. Yet, for every leader, this perspective is vital whether our ultimate circle includes millions or dozens. When navigating leadership storms, this accountability is an objective gauge we cannot ignore.[7]

Whether you are a pastor, politician, or police officer, it is imperative to remind yourself of the real consequences of a leadership disaster[8] and all the arenas of accountability that can give you perspective and keep you in flight.

Keys to Genuine Accountability

As we think about a fresh commitment to accountability, here are a few keys to making accountability work in your life.

1. Look for Providential Promptings

Many of the leaders mentioned in this chapter sensed God leading them to recognize the danger of "going it alone." In those moments, they become willing to risk their pride and self-preservation in order to enter into a genuine accountability. Executive Sid Verdoorn recognized a need for a "culture of accountability" for his employees. Missions leader Luis Bush embraced accountability under the press of incredible stress. Baseball Hall of Famer Paul Molitor turned to a trusted friend and locked into a lifestyle of covenantal friendship out of the darkest moment of his journey. Personally, I first pursued accountability as a young pastor dealing with complexities and attacks that almost drove me out of pastoral ministry.

We should look for God's promptings to be accountable to someone else. Paul Powers, a good friend and pastor of Union Baptist Church in Saint Johnsbury, Vermont, tells about a time a few years ago when he was deeply discouraged and planning to resign from vocational ministry. In his own words, he writes of the Lord orchestrating a breakthrough of accountability as he gathered with his small group.

> As we went through the meeting, I pretended all was well, but didn't contribute much. When we came to the prayer time, God kept reminding me of James 5:16, "Confess your trespasses to one another, and pray one for another, that you may be healed." I thought to myself, *I can't do this in this group; there are no spiritual giants in this room, only people I have led to Christ or helped on their spiritual journey. How can they help me?* But the thought persisted and I did not want to disobey God's promptings. So I briefly told the group of six to seven believers how discouraged I was and how close I was to quitting the ministry altogether.

When I finished, one man I had helped stood up and said to the group, "I think we need to put Pastor in the chair in the middle." We all knew what that meant. So I dutifully sat in the chair while these "common believers" prayed for me, their pastor. That broke the spell of discouragement and launched me on a road to recovery. It has been a long road, but I am so grateful for that moment and God's liberating power in my life through that group of "ordinary" believers. I still get tears of thankfulness to God for those people whenever I tell of that event.[9]

Pastor Powers adds, "Healthy, consistent accountability means being honest and open with one or more people about your struggles. The benefits are God's grace (James 4:6), which involves healing, deliverance, etc., and real biblical spiritual fellowship (Ephesians 4:25). I see vulnerability as a willingness to risk pride to obey God and enjoy the power of His grace."

Very often, God is orchestrating the call to vulnerability. We are wise to obey the call. It takes courage and wisdom—but the benefits are life changing.

2. Pursue Intentional Engagement

In seeking the right accountability partner(s), look for the following:

- *A person with proven character.* For me this has usually been a given, since the local church elders with whom I have served are required to demonstrate a lifestyle of exemplary commitment to integrity, family, and the truth of God's Word. Look for someone who is respected by a broad group of people and has demonstrated a balanced and faithful commitment to Christ.
- *A person with proven faithful service.* A servant's heart is evidenced in years of generous, selfless service. This kind of attitude makes accountability a blessing.
- *A person with a track record of healthy relationships.* Accountability can be very difficult with someone who carries the wounds of past hurts, distrust, and conflict. Major marriage, family, or friendship struggles are a sure-fire red light in selecting an accountability partner.

- *A person committed to mutual honesty and submission.* Because accountability is a two-way road, you want to select someone who is also willing to be vulnerable and can humbly receive honest input as well as give it. Look for evidence of this, not just a feeling that it could happen.

Set the goal of meeting weekly. With travel and vacations, you may not always achieve this, but a regular and consistent commitment will help keep you connected. Accountability is a big commitment but a vital one. It doesn't take long for your heart to veer off course or become overwhelmed by an unexpected crisis. Knowing you have a connection point with a trusted friend on a regular basis helps maintain the hope of finding support in the midst of life's storms.

Accountability should be more than a temporary therapy during crisis. It should be a lifestyle. In my early thirties I was scared into accountability as I cleaned up the mess of a moral failure in the church I was leading. I knew I just did not want to ever go through that kind of failure, so I pursued a weekly breakfast with the chairman of our elders. Each week, Bob and I met at Denny's restaurant. We spoke openly about our struggles, our time with God, our discouragements, our hopes, and our fears. Of course, we spoke extensively about ministry challenges. We prayed together. These mornings were an oasis to our souls. In a sense, Bob needed to learn to trust a pastor again. I needed to learn to trust someone with wisdom and conviction.

Since then, I have kept a commitment to consistent accountability. Every week I have been committed to meet with the chairman of the elders for heartfelt accountability. I remember life-changing moments with elders like Bob Ahmann, Gary Hess, Bud Mardock, Hal Wadley, Phil Dirksen, Dan Dunnmoyer, Frank DeLange, Russell Knight, Mike Pagh, and Rick Nelson. Their input has been a lifesaving gauge of objectivity that I treasure, even with tears, to this day.

3. Embrace the Risk of Trust

But there is risk in accountability. Not on the above list is one elder chairman who wounded me deeply. Donald (not his real name) became chairman of our elder team when the previous chairman had to retire. No strong candidates emerged, and Donald was selected by default, with considerable misgivings. He was a very bright man, but a man with unresolved hurts from his past church involvement and very strong views about how things should operate in the church. I reluctantly agreed to his selection and lived to regret it.

At our first weekly meeting, it was clear that Donald had numerous agendas with rigid expectations for my performance as pastor. He showed immediate signs of allowing the "chairman" title to go to his head. Our weekly meetings were more about debates and personal disconnects than about prayer and mutual enrichment.

Eventually he sought to remove me from the church when I did not comply with his controlling agenda for my life and for the ministry. In the midst of those months of deep pain, I thought many times about discontinuing my commitment to this kind of accountability. Yet, everything with reward also carries risk. As I look at the names, I realize that a ten-to-one ratio is not a bad proportion.

More importantly, the reward and enrichment of this accountability investment exponentially outweighs the pain of one elder's betrayal. Accountability is not always safe, but it is always worth it.

You will have to make this decision on your own. Consider the stakes of a leadership flight without accountability. Yes, there may be pain when accountability goes awry. Still, as a leader responsible for a planeload of human souls, you would be a fool to believe you can weather the storms of your responsibility with a Lone Ranger mentality.

4. Partner with the Holy Spirit

In John 16:12–15, Jesus spoke these fascinating words,

> I still have many things to say to you, but you cannot bear them now. However, when He, the Spirit of truth, has come, He will guide you into all truth; for He will not speak on His own authority, but whatever He hears He will speak; and He will tell you things to come. He will glorify Me, for He will take of what is Mine and declare it to you.

All things that the Father has are Mine. Therefore I said that He will take of Mine and declare it to you.

As Jesus describes the role of the Holy Spirit, one reality should become clear: Some truths are hard to understand or swallow apart from the wisdom of the Holy Spirit. In any relationship of accountability, it is vital to stay surrendered to the Holy Spirit in order to either receive or reject the input of others. The Holy Spirit gives us the ability to evaluate the input of others. The ultimate criterion for evaluating honest feedback is not if we like it, or if it makes us feel better. Rather, the question is, "Will this input help me better glorify Christ in my heart, attitudes, and behaviors?" This is always the goal of the Spirit's truth, written in the Word and often applied to our hearts with the help of loving, godly friends.

The scoreboard is in heaven.

DANIEL HENDERSON

*The great use of one's life is to spend it on something
that will outlast it, for the value of life is computed
not by its duration but by its donation.*

WILLIAM JAMES

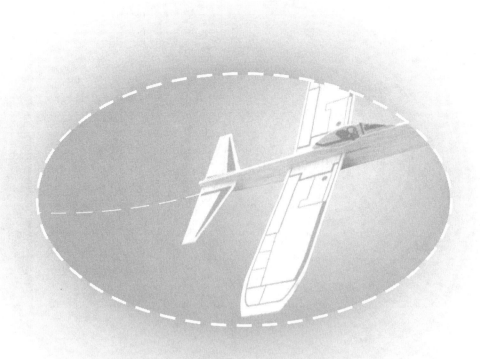

8

Eternal Significance

May 1, 1985, was the most difficult night of Vernon Brewer's life. During a lengthy surgery, doctors discovered and removed a five-pound cancerous tumor that was attached to his heart and lungs. In order to remove the mass, the surgeons took out approximately one-third of Brewer's left lung.

The news worsened the next day when Brewer learned that the doctors inadvertently severed the nerve to his vocal cords and diaphragm. He woke up unable to speak normally, barely able to muster a high-pitched whisper. For a man who made his living through speaking to audiences large and small, the situation seemed devastating. And then there was the cancer battle that loomed ahead.

"In one day, the security and normalcy of my entire world had disintegrated," Vernon recalled. "I had no idea that ahead of me was a battle that included eighteen surgeries and one and a half years of chemotherapy. All I knew as I lay in that hospital bed on May 1 was that my life had been turned upside down and it wasn't going to be righted any time soon."

During an eighteen-month struggle to survive cancer, Brewer developed a new commitment to the importance of prayer, a deeper appreciation for family and friends, and a whole new platform to minister to others.

Today, when he walks into the headquarters of World Help in Forest, Virginia, he passes these words stenciled in large letters across the main wall of the reception area: *Every day I try to live my life in such a way that I accomplish at least one thing that will outlive me and last for eternity.*

This statement defines all that Brewer does these days, even decades after the battle with cancer. As the founder and president of World Help, a nonprofit, nondenominational Christian organization that meets the spiritual and physical needs of hurting people around the world, he lives for the eternal impact. With his voice restored, he has led over five hundred local church evangelistic rallies, lectured on thirty college and university campuses, and conducted international evangelistic campaigns and rallies in over sixty-seven countries. In addition he has directed leadership training conferences in Uganda, China, India, Nepal, Burma, Romania, Russia, and Iraq.

Brewer says the bout with cancer left him with a constant—and healthy—eternal perspective. "It has caused me to evaluate each and every thing I do. It has forced me to ask the hard questions in life, to make sure I am spending what little time I have left on the important things—things that will last for eternity."

And Brewer concludes, "We must all remind ourselves each day of what is important to God and work toward accomplishing those things."[1]

The Scoreboard

I regularly tell myself and anyone else who will listen that "the scoreboard is in heaven." It may not take an extended battle with cancer or a brush with death, but somewhere along the way, every leader must learn to fix his eyes on the gauge where the real status of ministry and reward is captured. It is the gauge of eternal significance.

When Jesus said the first shall be last and the last shall be first (see Matthew 19:27–30), He was not just hypothesizing. When He noted that the impressive public prayers of the Pharisees would not be recognized in heaven, it was not just theory. When He said that a humble and simple cup of cold water given in His name would be rewarded, He was not kidding. Rather He was giving us a weighty warning that the eternal evaluation of our lives will be surprisingly different from the superficial scorekeeping of our earthly existence. The principle is essential for every life and every leader.

How else can you make sense of the riveting account in Matthew 7:21–23 where a cadre of great preachers, demon-exorcisers, and wonder-workers show up with full confidence at heaven's gate to celebrate their spiritual exploits only to learn that none of it mattered? In fact, they did not even make it into heaven, according to Jesus. You can't help but wonder how someone so active in making a "spiritual impact" could have been that confused about the things that count for eternity.

Calculating What Counts

Paul sheds light on this paramount concern as he describes the evaluation of lives and ministries in 1 Corinthians 3:11–15. Some of our Christian leadership accomplishments will be wood, hay, and stubble, burned into oblivion in the presence of the holy Christ. Other efforts will count as gold, silver, and precious stones, accompanied by lasting reward. What makes the difference? Paul clarifies, "The fire will test each one's work, of what sort it is" (v. 13).

It can be riveting to realize that the scoreboard is not about the outward size or earthly success of our efforts, but on the "sort" of work we have done. This focus on the quality, heart, and substance of our leadership helps us understand eternity's perspective on the work we do.

Speaking of this evaluation, Paul also notes that it involves Christ's judgment of the "secrets of men" (Romans 2:16). The sovereign and all-knowing Lord "will both bring to light the hidden things of darkness and reveal the counsels of the hearts. Then each one's praise will come from God" (1 Corinthians 4:5). He will look for a genuine faith that has been tested by the fire of adversity (1 Peter 1:7).

A key criterion will be whether our hearts have been motivated to please God, not ourselves or other people (2 Corinthians 5:9–10). I often say that if we please God, it does not matter whom we displease. If we displease God, it does not matter whom we please. The eternal scoreboard empowers us to live with this resolve.

- -

Where the Heart Is

An eternal perspective requires that we view our lives in terms of the motives within our hearts. The focus is on the quality of our leadership more than actual accomplishments that, in earthly terms, may be labeled "successes." The proper motive of our hearts, according to the Scriptures and when we face final judgment before the Lord, is to please our Father in heaven rather than people here on earth or ourselves. Paul puts it this way: "Our aim . . . [is] to be well pleasing to Him" (2 Corinthians 5:9).

- -

It seems clear that our eternal reward will not be about a superficial inspection of what we have done, but why we have done it and for whom. When it comes to leadership, we can do all the right things for all the wrong reasons. This is a powerful reality check and helps us understand what "scores" in heaven.

It is imperative to remember the things that matter on the eternal scoreboard as compared to our earthly measurements.

- Heaven measures by what is spiritual; we tend to evaluate things based on size.
- Heaven honors what is prayerful; we gravitate toward what is popular.
- Heaven honors the faithful; we honor the famous.
- Heaven honors the authentic; we seek to become affluent.
- Heaven will reveal the motive for our efforts; we measure the results in our efforts.

Of course, size, popularity, affluence, fame, and results are not inherently bad. They can, however, become hollow replacements for the things that really matter. We should intentionally and thoughtfully embrace the matters that matter in eternity.

Intersections of the Earthly and Eternal

So, with the scoreboard in mind, we are compelled to play the game differently here on earth. Knowing how the real score is kept motivates us to clarify the real rules. Not only does this enable us to avoid insignificant pursuits, but it also encourages us to recognize the eternal value of so much of what we do, even if the media, the crowd, the accountants, and the critics are unimpressed with our efforts.

TV producer and author Karen Covell serves as the director of the Hollywood Prayer Network. HPN seeks to mobilize prayer for "the most influential mission field in the world" through prayer intercessors around the world. This is more than a job for Karen. She and her husband, Jim (also a producer and my best friend in junior high school), have led a weekly prayer meeting in their home for their Hollywood colleagues for almost twenty-five years.

Not long ago, Karen discovered that a faithful friend and colaborer for over twenty years who handled HPN's finances was "borrowing money" from HPN. By the time Karen discovered this, it was almost too late to salvage the ministry. Suddenly she was in the situation of needing to decide how to handle her colleague and whether to save the ministry or just shut it down and start over. She found herself struggling with the thought of rebuilding—knowing the commitment, time, effort, and needed fund-raising that it would take.

In a recent interview she stated, "In my weariness, I wanted to give up. I questioned the purpose of the ministry and whether it would actually even be missed if I closed the doors and walked away. I then questioned whether anything I had done in the past decade had made any eternal difference and if it was all for naught. . . . I went through a desert."[2]

As Karen prepared for the next board of directors' meeting where she would have to present a response and resolution to this crisis, she was challenged by this Bible passage: "Never be lacking in zeal, but keep your spiritual fervor, serving the Lord. Be joyful in hope, patient in affliction, faithful in prayer. Share with God's people who are in need. Practice hospitality" (Romans 12:11–13 NIV).

She describes her response in this way, "It occurred to me that I don't have any choice. I *have* to keep fighting. I need to seek God to make sure I do it His way, but I realized that I was losing perspective on God's promise for me; that God had called me to this task years ago." It was during those days of prayer and new resolve that Karen affirmed her unique vision and calling, and the eternal significance of her work regardless of circumstances, critics, or crises.

Days later when she spoke to the HPN board, sharing her deep resolve, she began to weep. This is very uncharacteristic for Karen but reflected the fresh realization she felt about the eternal value of the mission. As she describes it, "My uncontrollable tears during that business meeting deepened my sense of purpose, my eternal significance, and my love for the Lord. The board reminded me that I am not the one to judge whether I'm being effective or if my work is making any difference. I am just supposed to keep my eyes on Jesus, show up each day, with spiritual fervor, and ask the Lord to do with me what He wants. And the rest is up to Him!"[3]

Karen Covell encountered an unprecedented storm in her leadership experience. By keeping her eye on the gauge of "eternal significance," she regained hope and resolve to continue in her obedience to the call. Her testimony echoes the assurance of Paul when he wrote, "For I know whom I have believed and am persuaded that He is able to keep what I have committed to Him until that Day" (2 Timothy 1:12).

Enemies of the Eternal "Win"

Every day, amid real-life decisions, the pull of surface evaluations and the noise of worldly standards seek to get us off course. As leaders, we must recognize the factors within us that can get our eyes off the gauge of eternal significance and put us in a tailspin toward feeling insignificant.

1. Apathy Fueled by Ignorance

Many leaders simply do not understand the power of the eternal scoreboard because they fail to grasp the clear biblical teaching on this issue. Ignorance is not bliss in this regard. Every leader must understand that "we must all appear before the judgment seat of Christ, that each one may receive the things done in the body, according to what he has done, whether good or bad" (2 Corinthians 5:10). This is not a judgment of sin, because the true child of God has already been forgiven (Romans 8:1). This is an evaluation of our life and works as a believer, as noted in the previous section of this chapter.

The rewards we receive are described as crowns (1 Corinthians 9:25; Philippians 4:1; 2 Timothy 4:8; James 1:12; 1 Peter 5:4). We will cast those crowns before Christ (Revelation 4:10) as an act of worship. Our crowns represent our capacity to give glory to Christ throughout eternity. It may sound a bit ethereal right now in the midst of e-mails to read, bills to pay, and projects to accomplish. Someday, it will be all that matters—and it will be forever.

2. Performance Fueled by Superficial Measurements

Superficial measurements of significance can create a performance-based approach to leadership. Most of us are trained to be overachievers by parents who overtly or even inadvertently communicate to us that our value is rooted in our accomplishments. Little League trophies, merit badges, academic recognitions, college scholarships, and penthouse offices may show our skills and determination, but they also can easily define and direct most of what we do. To right ourselves and have our motives in balance, we cannot ignore the gauge of eternal significance.

Reflecting on her own journey of understanding, Karen Covell notes, "Leaders are usually type-A personalities. We want success and we're not afraid to fight for it, believing that numbers, more finances, bigger membership, and a growing bottom line are proof of both our purpose and our success. It's a *lie* and so hard to fight against. Christians have embraced the world's measures of success and we expect one another to meet those in order to justify our ministry and its costs. This is damaging and causes us to push God out of the picture.

"I have to continually go back to the model of the first-century church when Christians worked with people one-on-one. The numbers in the crowds didn't prove success; it was the heart of the people they ministered to. Paul never compared himself with other servants of God; he told us to keep our eyes on the goal."[4]

3. Drivenness Fueled by Comparison

As Covell notes, in a leadership culture inundated by ads, promotion, and celebrity accomplishments, it is easy to allow subjective comparisons to drive our efforts. Comparison is an ugly game that no one ever wins. If we compare ourselves with others unfavorably, we become defeated and even jealous. If we compare ourselves favorably, we can become proud and condescending. Either way, we lose in eternity. As Paul says, those who are "measuring themselves by themselves, and comparing themselves among themselves, are not wise" (2 Corinthians 10:12).

After forty years of faithful leadership as the pastor of Arcade Baptist Church in Sacramento, California, Lee Tom prepared to retire. And so, in his retirement announcement, he cautioned his congregation as they looked for his successor with these wise words: "Never compare us, because you will only hurt both of us."

I was that successor and was grateful for his insightful concern during my eleven years at Arcade. Whenever we are motivated by surface comparisons, we have lost sight of the heart of New Testament leadership and service. As Vernon Brewer has learned, "It is so easy to get caught up in comparing ourselves to others, and by doing so, adapting a worldly view of success. We need to keep our focus on what God's view of success is."

4. Forgetfulness Fueled by Busyness

In his classic essay, "Tyranny of the Urgent," Charles Hummel recalled the caution that a cotton mill manager once told him: "Your greatest danger is letting the urgent things crowd out the important."

There is the familiar story of the three bricklayers who were approached by an inquisitive bystander one day as they were working. Each one of them was asked what they were doing. The first man answered gruffly, "I'm laying bricks." The second worker replied, "I'm putting up a wall." The third man said enthusiastically and with optimism, "I'm building a cathedral."

Leaders can easily get so overwhelmed by the duties, meetings, and deadlines that we forget what we are doing and why. With a mindful view of eternity, every task can be seen in terms of its impact on the lives of eternal souls and its advancement of an eternal mission.

Vernon Brewer speaks to us all when he notes, "Someday when you stand before God:

- He won't ask what kind of car you drove . . . He'll ask how many people you drove who did not have transportation.
- He won't ask the square footage of your house . . . He'll ask how many people you welcomed into your home.
- He won't ask about the clothes you had in your closet . . . He'll ask how many you helped to clothe.
- He won't ask what your highest salary was . . . He'll ask if you used it to further the kingdom of God.
- He won't ask what your job title was . . . He'll ask if you used your job to influence people for eternity.
- He won't ask how many friends you had . . . He'll ask how many people to whom you were a friend."[5]

Leaders who defy gravity are constantly reminding themselves that tasks can be translated into timeless impact with an intentional focus on the things that really count on heaven's scoreboard.

A New Way of Seeing

Helen Keller offers a powerful reminder at this point: "I can see, and that is why I can be happy, in what you call the dark, but which to me is golden. I can see a God-made world, not a man-made world." In a similar way, she noted, "It is a terrible thing to see and have no vision."[6]

Enduring and influential Christian leaders have at least one moment where they experience a powerful recalibration of vision. For Vernon Brewer, it was an eighteen-month struggle with cancer. For Karen Covell, it was a crisis within her organization. What has it been for you? Maybe you are in the midst of it now. If it has not occurred yet, pray for such vision. Your eternal influence depends on it.

As a college student, I traveled one summer with one of the school's singing teams. We visited several American churches before flying to the Pacific Rim for three weeks of ministry in Hong Kong, Taiwan, Japan, and South Korea.

I was assigned a solo part in a song titled "Looking through His Eyes," written by Mike Otto. As I sang this moving piece stateside, I really tried to get into it. I looked up on cue and even knelt during part of the performance that described a moment of kneeling with Jesus in the garden of Gethsemane and grieving for men who were headed to a hopeless eternity. Yet, in my heart it was just that—a performance. I began to pray, "God, teach me the meaning of this song."

Finally we departed for Hong Kong, South Korea, Japan, and Taiwan. During our weeks in these countries, I saw and felt many things. Yet it was not until our final day when we were touring a Buddhist temple in Taipei that the power of the message hit me. As I observed a grandmother teaching her grandchildren to throw down two pieces of wood to determine Buddha's will for their lives, I was struck by the eternal destiny of souls without Christ. Watching scores of people bowing before the potbellied idol deepened my brokenness in that moment.

That day, I realized that I had to learn to look beyond superficial appearances of clothing, houses, cars, and even culture. God gave me eyes to see eternal souls in need of His eternal truth. I would never sing "Looking through His Eyes" again without understanding the power of the words. I vowed to never lead again without endeavoring to do so with an eternal perspective. The song's last line reminds me of what all leaders longing for an eternal perspective must do: "For if once I could see this world the way You see, I just know I'd serve You more faithfully."

When we commit to the gauge of an eternal perspective, we will have a recalibrated, accurate vision. And our hearts shall resonate with Paul's when he wrote, "So we fix our eyes not on what is seen, but on what is unseen. For what is seen is temporary, but what is unseen is eternal" (2 Corinthians 4:18 NIV).

*The family circle is the
supreme conductor of Christianity.*

HENRY DRUMMOND
Minister, professor, and author

*Husbands, likewise, dwell with them with understanding,
giving honor to the wife, as to the weaker vessel,
and as being heirs together of the grace of life,
that your prayers may not be hindered.*

1 PETER 3:7

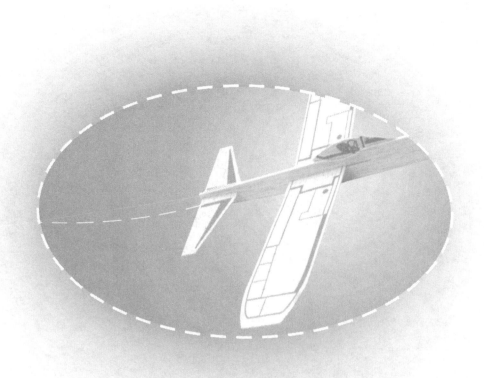

9

Gauge Seven:

Healthy Family Life

Few things are more rewarding than carrying out your calling as a leader, knowing that it is not your top priority, but assured that the things that matter most are in proper order—like your heart and your home. Conversely, there is nothing more draining than trying to effectively fulfill your leadership duties, knowing that your heart is empty and your home is broken.

In aviation, the marital status and family function of a pilot are not major factors in one's ability to fly a plane. In Christian leadership, a healthy family life is a requirement for effective and enduring flight. Character and relationships matter more than training and skills.

Often those who suffer the most during and after a leadership crash are the very ones who could have contributed the most to its prevention. Many leadership disasters are connected to an unhealthy marriage and a dysfunctional family life. A wholesome marriage—and authentic, loving family relationships—should be priorities. Addressing family difficulties is crucial for a leader who wants to soar over the long haul.

Significantly, when the apostle Paul spells out the biblical qualifications for leaders in the church, he lists marital fidelity, effective household management, and respectful children as essential. As the text reminds us, "For if a man does not know how to rule his own house, how will he take care of the church of God?" (1 Timothy 3:5). Whether in full-time ministry, business, education, or any other field, authentic Christian leadership requires a large, clear, and frequently consulted gauge that indicates the proper function of family life.

Reality Check

Dennis Henderson has been in full-time pastoral ministry for over forty years. He frequently speaks to business groups on motivational issues of purpose and self-management, but serves full-time as senior pastor of Sherman Bible Church in Sherman, Texas. A high-energy leader, Dennis accomplishes a lot; yet there have been seasons when his productivity undermined his family. More than once his home was on what he describes as the "ledge of destruction."

His first family crisis occurred over thirty years ago while on staff at a megachurch. At the time he was averaging sixteen to eighteen hours a day, seven days a week, in the ministry. Each week also required two to three days of travel away from home in ministry assignments related to his job. His wife, Billie, recalls that during one year from August 1 to December 25, he had been home one evening.

One day when they were able to go Christmas shopping together, Dennis made a comment that hurt his wife. He recalls: "While shopping I said, 'I feel like I am wasting time.' It was a crushing moment. I was so engrossed in ministry that I did not even realize how that came across.

"To add to the problem, there was an expectation in that ministry that one could not turn back once they became a stellar performer."

After three and a half years at this pace and great pain in his family, Dennis recognized his commitment to work was far beyond the call of God. He realized his own desire to move ahead in ministry had entrapped him in what was actually a sinful pattern of life that violated God's priorities. "I found my ministry getting larger, but my heart getting smaller. In fact, my heart had almost died. I had become a machine that produced ministry activity without any sense of God. It was fine for the organization as the job was getting done, but a deep pit of emptiness of soul had overtaken my life. My wife was suffering greatly yet without complaining. I finally slowed down over a Christmas break long enough to hear the Holy Spirit reveal my bizarre lifestyle."

As Dennis dealt with his heart and analyzed the situation, he realized there was no way to change the level of activity now that he had laid an expectation of performance. The only option left was to resign. In the next six months Dennis took the appropriate steps and left that ministry without causing harm to it. "But great harm had taken place in my family and personal life," he notes. "I had to finally determine that my obedience to God, my heart, and my home were of greater value than the size and scope of a ministry."[1]

There would be other occasions when he would fall into a similar trap of overwork at the expense of marriage and family. Each time he learned deeper and better lessons about himself, his marriage, and his priorities.

By God's grace Dennis and Billie have been married more than forty-five years and are experiencing the best years of their life and ministry together. On their seventeen-acre ranch, they have a facility called "Monday Morning" designed to help struggling leadership marriages.[2] Their journey and the painful lessons they've learned have translated into grace-giving wisdom and care for many other leadership couples trapped in a pattern of neglect and dysfunction.

The Need for Balance

In working with other leaders, Henderson has learned about their need for balance. "Leaders are normally strong personalities. They have a desire to make a difference. Leaders are many times extremist in their personality and activities. Thus, leadership becomes the extreme. The pressure to succeed placed on them by themselves or by those around them pushes them beyond responsible balance. At a high pace, many times the quiet of time with God slips away. The heart becomes cold. The feet run fast and the knees seldom bend in prayer."

As he often reminds those who come to Monday Morning for help,

"Family is a big part of the life message of a leader. His ability is not nearly as important as his example and model. His family speaks louder than his position or personality. His credibility is beyond his leadership of systems, strategies, and vision-casting. Family validates or discounts all other activities of a leader."[3]

Dennis's story echoes that of many leaders. It is easy to fall into a pattern of being driven at work and preoccupied with success to the point of neglecting primary relationships at home, putting at risk everything that really matters. Sometimes the narcotic of activity even numbs us to the carelessness of our approach and destruction we are causing at home.

Don't miss the key factor of this story. When Dennis realized his life was losing altitude, he took a long look at the family gauge and made a major midcourse correction that involved a job change, relocation, and a fresh start. A leader *can* make such a change. A radical decision? Yes. But it's a wise decision, for all of a leader's current effectiveness and family well-being are the fruit of developing a healthy family life.

What the Gauge Tells Us

The readings of the "family" gauge on the leadership instrument panel are not complex—but they are compelling. They demand substantive time and rapt attention.

As a pastor for over twenty-five years, the husband of one wife for almost thirty years, and the father of three children who are walking in truth and serving Christ, I am most blessed. But now a confession: There were days when I wanted to bail on ministry, walk out the door of the home, give my children one-way tickets to anywhere, and simply cash it in. I took none of these actions—and God has helped us keep our family together. But it has taken a lot of time and much-focused attention on the gauge. It will require the same attention—and seeking God's mercy—for you. Watch the family gauge!

From my own experience, I have found that six primary messages decorate the "functional family gauge":

1. Christ is first.
2. Satan stalks.
3. Marriage matters.
4. Children count.
5. Family requires focus.
6. Importing precedes exporting (see p. 127 ff.).

When we are watchful and careful with these six message markers on the family gauge, not only do we reap the rewards of a rich home life, but we build the kind of relationships that provide vital feedback for our professional leadership. Everyone wins.

1. Christ Is First.

The ultimate priority of a vibrant relationship with Christ is the life-source for families that last. As important as spouses, children, homes, and family memories can be, they do not define our lives—Christ does. Only as He is first in the heart of a leader can that leader's family truly experience spiritual and emotional health. As one writer put it, "Living in a time when the family is under attack, the real danger is idolizing the family. We hear 'the family first' and may be tempted to say 'amen.' But Jesus will have none of this. When the family is first, God plays second fiddle."[4]

2. Satan Stalks.

The *Far Side* cartoon says it all. Two buck deer stand in the woods engaged in conversation. One has a target on his chest as the other comments, "Bummer of a birthmark, Hal." Leaders are special targets of the Enemy. The birthmark comes with the calling. Family members are also in the Enemy's scope. Experience tells me he seldom uses a rifle but prefers a machine gun in his attack strategy. If Satan cannot take out the primary leader, he will go after the spouse and children. He hates the powerful impact of godly leaders, healthy homes, loving spouses, and spiritually capable children. Few things are more strategic in advancing the kingdom of Christ than a functional, spiritually fruitful family.

My friend Ted was on a plane flying to San Jose, California, several years ago. During the flight, a gentleman seated next to him appeared to be praying. This sparked some curiosity with Ted. The meal came (back when they served free meals), and the man would not eat. Before the plane landed, Ted inquired curiously, "You look like you've been praying on this flight." The man responded, "Yes, I have." He asked the gentleman, "Are you fasting also?" And again he responded, "Yes, I am." Ted smiled. "You must be a Christian."

The man looked back sternly and said, "Absolutely not!"

"Then what is this all about?" Ted asked. "Why are you fasting and praying?"

With a very serious look on his face, the man responded, "I am a satanist, and once a week, satanists across the country have vowed together to pray for the downfall of the marriages of Christian leaders."

Was this guy legitimate? I don't know. Is this scenario possible? Absolutely. Is it consistent with what we know about the Devil's schemes? Sure. Does it put us on high alert as we lead, protect, and pray for our families? It should.

3. Marriage Matters.

I've heard it said that the best gift a leader can give his organization is a healthy marriage. Of course, within the home nothing is more important to the stability and well-being of the family than the condition of your marriage.

This chapter does not permit me to offer a crash course on strengthening your marriage. But, very simply, a leader (speaking to husbands in particular) must model Christ's love in his marriage. This does not depend on the temperament, spirituality, or responsiveness of the spouse. This is about the character of Christ ruling the heart and living through the leader in his home. It must be supernatural because no leader, left to himself, can do this. My definition of this love is, "an act of self-sacrifice, flowing from the heart, produced by the Holy Spirit for the good of others and the glory of God."

Again, on this front, the Enemy is always working his sly designs. He wants to harden the heart of a husband toward the unique needs of his wife. I know this firsthand. God has blessed me with a wonderful wife and a good marriage. However, I have found there are those special times when I need a 2 x 4 board across the head to wake me up and get me refocused on the priority of marriage.

One evening during the opening session of a national prayer conference, my friend Bob Bakke, who leads the North America Global Day of Prayer effort, helped direct a season of prayer. As I sat, praying and listening, I had an "ah-ha" moment that changed my life. God brought to my attention the truth of 1 Peter 3:7, "Husbands, likewise, dwell with them with understanding, giving honor to the wife, as to the weaker vessel, and as being heirs together of the grace of life, that your prayers may not be hindered."

Suddenly, I realized that even though I had a primary calling to mobilize prayer in the church, the Enemy was working overtime to slowly destroy my ministry by hardening my heart toward the desires of my wife. Rather than understanding her important needs, I was resenting them. Rather than giving her honor as the weaker vessel, I was putting her in the background because she did not meet my expectations. Rather than being heirs of grace, we were obstructing God's full provision for our marriage through apathy and neglect. The Devil loved it so—because my prayers were being hindered at the personal, family, and ministry levels.

That night I wept in deep repentance and resolved to get my heart right with the Lord and my wife. A few days later, I also sought the forgiveness of my children for my foolishness in failing to be the husband I needed to be—and in allowing the Enemy to so cunningly take advantage of my heart and home. It was a turning point in our marriage and family, and in my leadership.

In a similar moment, I was sitting with a good friend at a recent Men's Prayer Summit when he looked me in the eye and asked a very direct question. He inquired, "Does Rosemary really *know* that she is more important to you than your ministry? If so, how do you demonstrate it?" My answer was acceptable, but his questions lingered with me and prompted some very positive changes in my attitude and approach.

This kind of honesty tends to refocus a leader on this primary relationship of life. Every leader needs truth input to keep him focused in the matter of his marriage. The spousal relationship is a core human relationship. It either sets a trajectory of wholeness and authenticity or becomes a growing cancer of a disingenuous life.

4. Children Count.

The roles and responsibilities of a leader in his home are clear. As a father, he is to provide for family/children (2 Corinthians 12:14) and ensure proper nurture and discipline (Ephesians 6:4; Colossians 3:21; Hebrews 12:6). Mothers are to raise their children in faith and love (1 Timothy 2:15) and manage the home (1 Timothy 5:14). The children are to live in obedience to parents (Ephesians 6:1–3; Colossians 3:20) and care for parents in old age (1 Timothy 5:8).

Beyond these duties, I recommend some very practical commitments that help the parent/child environment and relationship to flourish. As the last verse of the Old Testament describes the work of God in the coming of Christ, He would "turn the hearts of the fathers to the children, and the hearts of the children to their fathers" (Malachi 4:6). A healthy family goes beyond mere duty to a discovery of a true heart connection.

Here are four *I*s that can help you develop a true heart connection to your children. First, a leader should *intimately know* his children. A cookie-cutter approach to child rearing never works, as each child is a uniquely designed gift from the hand of a creative God. The kind of communication that facilitates this knowledge of your children's personalities and gifts has to be intentional and consistent. It will take time.

Once when my children were young, a friend told me what he did to capture quality conversation with his kids: The family sat together in a hot tub. He described how that environment facilitated a lot of free-flowing interaction (no pun intended) as everyone sat in the warm, bubbling water with nothing to do but talk. I tried it; we bought our own hot tub, and I still remember many of the conversations that followed, conversations with each of my children that really allowed me to know and understand them. In many ways, their life choices were the fruit of these deep conversations— not always in the hot tub but often there. It may not be a Cal-Spa for you and your family, but every leader must find that place and time that allows him to dial in to the real heart of each child.

Second, a leader must also *invest* in his children, based on their needs and interests. Again, this requires time and attention. For one of our children, it was coaching a Little League sports team. For another, it was going

---

The Four *I*s for a Heart Connection with Your Children

Here are four *I*s that will help you know your children better:

1. *Intimately* know your children. Each child has a unique personality and distinct gifts. Be intentional and consistent in spending time with them so you can know them intimately.
2. *Invest* in your children. Observe and, at times, participate in their activities so they know you care. This can be sports, music, speech, or art. Wherever their interests lie, be there to support them.
3. *Include* your children in your own life activities. Look for creative ways to let your children participate in various activities. This can include inviting them to the office when appropriate and combining out of town/state business trips and conferences with vacation; you pay their way and join them on breaks during your trip and then continue with them on vacation when the business portion is complete. Let them see you as a leader/employee; they will get a better understanding of responsibility and what Dad (or Mom) does.
4. *Inspire* your children through example. Your godly pursuits and genuine heart for God's people inspire them to honor God. And your loving actions and words toward their mother will let them know that love counts. They are watching your actions and character. By God's grace you can inspire them to integrity and endurance.

---

to drum lessons and attending concerts. For another, it was dance classes and tuning in to art interests.

Third, the wise leader learns to also *include* his children in his own life. No doubt, there are not enough hours in the day to do a perfect job at balancing work and family. However, a dose of creativity can help cultivate opportunities. In my earlier years, there were those times when I was required to go back into the office to work late. Rather than leaving my children at home, I would bring them with me. We would arrive with blankets, pillows, popcorn, and their favorite video games or movies in hand. This "campout" became one of the great memories my children have. Rather than my office being some "black hole" where Dad disappeared at night, they remember it as a fun place where we would have some great activities they enjoyed. Of course, after they fell asleep I got my work done. It was a win-win.

In another case, I was assigned to some extraordinary travel for the Baptist association to which our church belonged. The national office allocated some money for our church to bring in some high-quality preachers to fill the pulpit on the Sundays I would be absent. Instead, I asked them to recategorize those funds to allow me to take my wife and children on some of the trips. I knew our staff could help fill the pulpit, but my family needed time with me. The organization agreed.

The kids especially remember these travels with great affection. I intentionally selected venues where we could add some great experiences to the trip (on our own nickel), which included professional sports games, Disney World, beaches, and other notable sites. The key is they felt a part of Dad's life.

Fourth, a leader should *inspire* his children. He can inspire them to love by loving their mother. He can inspire them to honor God by his example of godly pursuits. He can inspire them to serve by his genuine heart for God's people and mission in the world. He can inspire them to integrity and endurance by keeping his eyes on the instrument panel during the inevitable storms of life. In time, they will inspire him in return.

5. Family Requires Focus

Most of us think the important tasks of the day occur when we arrive at the office. While those duties are important, the priority obligations really occur when we walk in the door of the home at the end of the workday.

Over the years I've used the idea of praying on the way home for family members, imagining ahead of time how I should minister to each one. I've even knelt outside the door prior to entering the house, asking God to help me remember that my real ministry of the day was about to begin.

Such focus begins with our spouse, even after a challenging day in ministry. Ken Nair, author of *Discovering the Mind of a Woman*, dispels the notion that men cannot understand women, which is often an excuse for neglect of domestic responsibilities. Because every man has the mind of Christ, he *can* understand his wife and give proper attention to her needs.

He writes, "Ask yourself, 'What do I typically say and do when I walk into the house after a hard day at the office?'" Then Nair elaborates,

> When was the last time you made your wife a priority as you entered your house, embracing her, giving her more than a glancing peck on the cheek? When was the last time you asked "How did your day go?" And then you stuck around, concentrating on her answer, even if it took a while and disrupted your schedule. When was the last time she felt your heart reach out to her with a question like "What was the toughest thing that happened to you today?" If you are Christlike and convinced that she is more important than you are (Phil. 2:3), your first concern when you walk in the house will not be that your needs are met. You will be concerned that your wife and children know that you are thinking of *them* first when you walk through the door.[5]

6. Importing Precedes Exporting

I heard John Maxwell speak at a Promise Keepers conference some years ago, and one statement still stands out: "If it doesn't work at home, don't export it." In my view, the "it" he is referring to is relational authenticity. The work of Christ's kingdom advances on relationships. A leader must understand that genuine relationships begin at home

The home is the primary laboratory of relationships. Home is the ultimate 24/7 reality show of life. There is no professional pretense in the home. Titles, office size, education, "org charts," and the complexity of one's schedule are completely unimpressive inside the walls of the home. Responsive and responsible relationships are the language of home life. But the context is often raw—certainly rewarding, but raw. What a man is at home, a man is.

Here are four elements a leader should import into his home.

First, we must import *honesty*. For the family gauge to work properly, honesty about feelings and failures, hopes and hurts, dreams and disappointments must be cultivated. Again, the leader serves himself and his family well when he learns to listen for honest input and encourage feedback. "Faithful are the wounds of a friend" (Proverbs 27:6)—and fruitful are the wounds of family members.

Second, we must be open to the need to import *humility*. Lead by being humble before your spouse and children. Over the years in my role as pastoral counselor, I have felt the frustration of family members, spouses in particular, who wanted to see change in their home but were blocked from the needed breakthrough by an unwillingness of a strong personality (usually the husband) to admit the need for input and correction. It is indeed humbling to admit that your marriage is struggling and that you need help. It is humbling to learn your spouse or one of your children has a solid suggestion or spots a mistake you make.

Remember, God resists the proud (James 4:6), but He always finds ways to get grace into the hearts of humble people, including humble leaders. He can and will do that at times through family members.

Third, such humility may lead us to import *help*. Leaders often get help from a doctor when they are sick. They seek expertise from other leaders when facing a conundrum at work. They get advice on home improvement and perfecting their golf game. Yet, marriage and family are much more important than any of these.

Numerous times as a pastor, I have sought the wisdom and objective input of a counselor. My wife and I have benefited from retreat centers designed to specifically help pastoral couples. I've sought professional input on challenges with my kids. No doubt, I have been helped in many meaningful ways as a result. I am so grateful I did not allow the pride of position or pomposity of theological learning to stand in the way of my need for help from wise and caring people who can see things from a different perspective.

Fourth, we need to import *heart reconnection* as we get healthy. Families need to do life with hearts wide-open. Laughing together, playing together, grieving together, weeping together, praying together, and worshiping together—all are heart-healthy activities. It's more than just being in the same room; it's about being on the same page emotionally.

For type-A leaders (like the present writer), this is a learned but essential skill. I still remember watching a movie about a dying woman one December afternoon with my wife. It made us both think of her mother, who had passed away eight months earlier. A few minutes later, we stood in the kitchen in tears, embracing each other with a heart connection that was all about how we both missed her sweet mother so much and were still grieving—together. These moments are priceless and must be pursued with a passion for the sake of a healthy home.

Export Health

When you import the right things into the home, you can export real *health*. A healthy family is at the core of healthy living, healthy leadership, and healthy influence beyond the walls of the home.

As my children are now establishing their own homes and careers, I am thrilled to see how they are carrying the values and attitudes of our home environment into other settings—and to a new generation. In a sense, they have become "missionaries of family health" to friends and coworkers. While far from perfect, your children can become a living tribute to the health you seek to develop in your home. Their lives can bring great joy to your hearts as parents. In spite of our many mistakes, your children eventually can move on to export what your spouse and you have taught them by the grace of Christ.

The Mark of Lasting Influence

Doug Boquist, pastor of Bedford Church of the Nazarene in Bedford, Ohio, recounts a time when he was feeling a definite leading to make a change in his ministry focus—not for negative reasons but in response to a deep stirring in a particular direction. Knowing it could be traumatic for the family, he almost whimsically asked his wife: "Well, if we're leaving and we could pick anywhere in the country to minister next, where would you like to live?"

Doug describes her response with these words, "I'll never forget her answer. Without hesitation she said: 'Wherever you are.' Like a refreshing glass of water on a hot, sticky day, my wife's words brought comfort and direction. We were going to be leaving a place of ministry that we loved, but we were going to move on together. Our family was intact. Our four children were serving the Lord. Our marriage was strong."[6]

Doug's testimony reflects the life of a leader who kept his eye on the family gauge. By importing honesty, humility, help, and heart connections, he was able to enjoy health at home and work, even in times of stressful redirection.

Pastor Boquist adds this reminder for fellow leaders: "It is a constant temptation to allow the 'metrics' of our work to determine our sense of significance. When a leader forgets the source of his significance, these metrics take on an overpowering influence. Looking back on twenty-five years of leadership, I realize now that too many times I surrendered my identity to the surface numbers and results. I've come to realize that my position as a faithful husband and father is the moral authority on which I dare minister to my Father's other children.

"I am absolutely convinced that what happens in my home, with my own children, will far exceed the influence I will ever have as a leader of other people."

The best leaders limp.

DANIEL HENDERSON

*Though He was a Son, yet He learned obedience
by the things which He suffered.*

HEBREWS 5:8

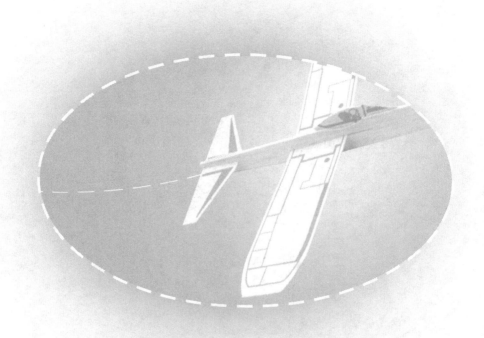

10

Gauge Eight:

Indispensable Pain

One of my early shockers as a young pastor was the amount of time I spent helping couples in crisis. I had not heard the grim statistics on the divorce rates among believers and was stunned that so many marriages were in deep trouble through constant conflict and even long-term bitterness between husbands and wives.

For perspective, I sought the counsel of an older, wiser, and very experienced Christian counselor in our church named Ron. As I communicated the burden I carried on behalf of these troubled couples, Ron offered an insight I never forgot. He explained, "The basic problem with these couples, and the majority of American Christians, is that they have no theology of suffering." He continued, "They are not committed to endure hardship and difficult pain, in marriage or any other area of their lives. As a result, they just 'bail' rather than stay in the fight to learn the lessons God wants them to learn for the sake of their own character development."

It's not just couples who must learn a theology of suffering. Leaders who last also must adopt a strong theology of suffering. Certainly this can be cognitively understood from biblical teachings on hardship and endurance.

Ultimately, it has to be enfolded into the fabric of the leader's soul through the crucible of personal suffering.

Leading through Loss

Wayne and Jennifer Dean were husband and wife who eventually became partners in ministry and leadership. Jennifer has served for many years as the founder and lead teacher for The Praying Life Foundation. After many years of successful work in the corporate world, Wayne decided to take a huge leap of faith and leave his secular career to be a full-time manager and president of the ministry. As Jennifer describes Wayne's dramatic shift: "He put all his skills and his experience and his personal people skills to work running The Praying Life Foundation. No paycheck. No company car. No company trips. Just three little boys and a wife he believed in."

She describes their partnership with these words, "This ministry of mine is ours. We grew it from a corner of our dining room to a full-time ministry with office and employees and volunteers. Side by side. Praying together through every decision, every opportunity, every redirection along the way."

In October 2005, Wayne and Jennifer met with Wayne's doctor about what had been diagnosed as an inner ear infection. Instead, they heard the dreadful news that Wayne had an advanced case of an aggressive brain cancer, for which there was essentially no hope of cure. Two months later, Wayne died. It was December 13, two weeks before Christmas.

Jennifer describes her pain and loss this way:

When the fog lifted, and I began to realize that I was a *widow*, of all things—I could not imagine continuing in the ministry. It had always been "us," never just "me." The thought of taking on a new project or coming up with a fresh thought seemed impossible. I couldn't say a whole sentence without breaking into sobs. The first year of my widowhood was excruciating. I couldn't leave my house because I never knew what memory might ambush me and send me into a tailspin right in public. I started explaining to my friends and my sons, "A widow lives in my body and I don't know her. I don't know how she'll act. I don't know what to expect from her. I can't let her out in public."[1]

Eventually the Lord's grace transformed her wounds into triumph as she began to understand the value of her pain. "I am just through my third year of widowhood," Jennifer told me during a recent interview. "I feel like myself again. The widow and I have integrated. I'm not fragile anymore, but now I can be patient with others who are fragile."

Jennifer offers this insight into the redeeming value of pain: "If we cherish our comfort and value our status quo, then we can never let pain in to do its transforming work. If we resent the intrusion of crucifixion, then we will never experience the wonder of resurrection."

A Powerful Leadership Indicator

C. S. Lewis said, "God whispers to us in our pleasures, speaks to us in our conscience, but shouts in our pain: It is His megaphone to rouse a deaf world."[2] Pain is God's way of awakening and shaping leaders as well. It may seem a strange component on the leadership instrument panel, but seasoned and enduring leaders always have stories of pain and loss that have powerfully shaped their character, approach, and longings.

I've heard it said that before God can use a man greatly, He must first wound him deeply. Oswald Chambers was right when he taught, "If we are ever going to be made into wine, we will have to be crushed—you cannot drink grapes. Grapes become wine only when they have been squeezed."[3] Charles Spurgeon understood this when he wrote, "I am certain that I never did grow in grace one-half so much anywhere as I have upon the bed of pain."[4]

That Strange Flight Gauge Called Pain

Of the nine gauges of the leadership instrument panel, none may be more surprising nor paradoxical than pain. It may be indispensable, but it is rarely welcome. Yet God uses it for good. Consider these paradoxical truths about the role of pain in our lives:

- Wounds are the preface to true greatness.
- Before God can remake us, He must first break us.
- Leaders tested by adversity are able to understand and minister to those they serve.
- Authentic, high-impact ministry results from an honest admission of the hard-earned lessons of life.
- Before you bless, you must bleed; before you can help, you must first hurt.
- Our wounds become tender scabs but later empowering scars. Through our wounds God notarizes our leadership as true and authoritative.

Eventually leaders learn from experience that before God can remake us, He must first break us. The truly lasting lessons are learned through suffering. Wounds are the preface to true greatness. Just a few of the many biblical examples convince us:

- Job lost his family and fortunes and endured painful misunderstanding from friends before he was blessed with a deeper knowledge of God and the restoration of his life.
- Joseph was rejected by family and forgotten in a prison he did not deserve before he saved the day for Egypt.
- Moses endured the desert in forty years of obscurity and bewilderment before he became the great leader of Israel's deliverance.

- David ran for his life many years, facing painful rejection and perplexing delays, before he became Israel's king.
- Hosea endured the pain of repeated infidelity after marrying a prostitute before he became a powerful prophet.
- Peter felt the regret and brokenness of his own failed loyalty before he preached with power at Pentecost.
- Paul was blind, broken, and banished on the back side of a desert in preparation for his world-changing ministry of church planting and inspired biblical writing. He became even stronger through the weakness of a nagging thorn in his flesh.

The Value of the Wound

If wounds precede greatness, Pastor Jeff Wells has become a very effective leader through his previous years of deep and desperate pain. He leads WoodsEdge Community Church in Woodlands, Texas, a congregation of over 4,500 people at three sites.

Early in his adult life, Jeff was diagnosed with a severe case of obsessive-compulsive disorder. He had become a world-class marathon runner yet was constantly gripped by bizarre thoughts of falling or failing in an important race. And as a young pastor, he was plagued with doubts about his very salvation and deep struggles to even feel loved by God.

At the end of a seven-year period, his struggle had become intense, and he undertook what he calls a "desperate quest."

"This was the ball game for me," Wells notes. "I had come to a point where I [wanted to] know and feel the love and tender mercy of God. I prayed desperately out of my weakness, brokenness, and vulnerability."

Embarrassing as it was, Wells shared his struggle with some praying friends. He also learned to worship God in His love and grace, even with daily singing. Eventually, from his brokenness in prayer, study, and worship, Wells was substantially healed by God.

Today he shares his journey openly with his church and every new members class. "God used this pain to produce a depth in my life. I would not have it any other way. When you suffer so badly for so many years, you gain a whole different perspective on life and ministry."[5]

I cannot presume to understand the reasons God allows these wounds for people like Jeff and others He chooses to use. Still, the value of wounds must be fully embraced by leaders who expect to stay in flight. In this light, it is encouraging to understand some of the rather obvious and indispensable benefits of pain.

1. Dependence

For Pastor Wells, the pursuit of wholeness has continued to this day, even though much healing occurred many years ago. Every week he leads a prayer service when his congregation declares their dependence on Christ. The heart God wants to shape in us through our wounds is the heart that cries out, "I need Thee, oh I need Thee. Every hour, I need Thee." This cry of dependence is branded on Wells's heart.

Widow Jennifer Dean also recognizes this need for dependence. "I realize that the great wound inflicted on my heart has made me desperately dependent on God in a way I would never have known otherwise, but that has transformed my ministry and given it a new depth."

A. W. Tozer described the difficult process and deep value of spiritual desperation:

> All great Christians have been wounded souls. It is strange what a wound will do to a man. Here's a soldier who goes out to the battlefield. He is full of jokes and strength and self-assurance; then one day a piece of shrapnel tears through him and he falls, a whimpering, beaten, defeated man. Suddenly his whole world collapses around him and this man, instead of being the great, strong, broad-chested fellow that he thought he was, suddenly becomes a whimpering boy again. And such have ever been known, I am told, to cry for their mothers when they lie bleeding and suffering on the field of battle. There is nothing like a wound to take the self-assurance out of us, to reduce us to childhood again and make us small and helpless in our own sight.[6]

2. Fruitfulness

Of course, Jesus invited us to understand that real fruitfulness comes from this desperate dependence and a spirit of humble helplessness. He teaches, "I am the vine, you are the branches. He who abides in Me, and I in him, bears much fruit; for without Me you can do nothing" (John 15:5). Yet His commitment to our fruit bearing is relentless and can involve difficult situations for the sake of our growth. In John 15:2 He said, "Every branch that bears fruit He prunes, that it may bear more fruit."

Fruit-bearing branches are not coddled, sheltered, or preserved in some museum of faith. Rather, they get pruned. This "cutting back" is painful but necessary for the sake of bearing more and greater fruit. Great fruit is a surefire mark of growing leadership. Yet, it always comes with a price tag.

3. Empathy

The positive impact of Jesus' empathetic heart toward His followers is clear. Hebrews 4:15–16 tells us, "For we do not have a High Priest who cannot sympathize with our weaknesses, but was in all points tempted as we are, yet without sin. Let us therefore come boldly to the throne of grace, that we may obtain mercy and find grace to help in time of need."

Similarly, leaders who have been tested through adversity have an ability to understand and minister to those they serve. Whether it is a hurting colleague at the office, a bereaved employee, or a brokenhearted parishioner, each is encouraged to trust Christ for mercy and grace by our own story of Christ's work in our lives.

Pastor Wells describes this benefit. "The people need to know about our wounds. Some are overwhelmingly struggling with mental disease and emotional problems. They know I understand pain—even their kind of pain. It brings a rapport, trust, and authenticity to the culture of our ministry." Similarly, Jennifer Dean observes, "Those we lead and influence suffer. They have suffered, they will suffer, and they are suffering. Unless we can display our wounds, others can't see the benefit of pain and the power of His resurrection."

4. Authentic Impact

Barely forty years old, I was not sure I had a lot to share when I was asked to serve as the national spokesman in 1999 for our association of churches. My assignment included traveling a couple of times a month and speaking at pastors conferences to encourage pastors' hearts and challenge their faith.

I soon recognized the message with greatest impact was a story of pain—my own story of brokenness and the lessons learned as I fought to keep my joy in the midst of difficulty. Speaking from Hebrews 13:17, I noted the constant challenge of ministering among hurting people who hurt other people, including their leaders. In time I had learned the hard lessons of what it meant to lead "with joy and not with grief," knowing joyless, defeated leaders are described as "unprofitable" to the people. And I've learned that authentic, high-impact ministry results from an honest admission of the hard-earned lessons of life.

So each time I preached, I closed the message with a piece of poetry titled, "The Wound." I had written this piece with tears at the end of a painful season of ministry. Years later, pastors and their spouses still catch me at conferences and show me their copy of "The Wound," usually tucked permanently in their Bibles. (You can read "The Wound" at the end of this book.)

Rick Warren affirms this kind of impact when he writes in his best-selling *The Purpose Driven Life*, "At some point in your life you must decide whether you want to impress people or influence people. You can impress people from a distance, but you must get close to influence them, and when you do that, they will be able to see your flaws."[7] I've heard it said that before you can bless, you must bleed; before you can help, you must first hurt.

5. Christlikeness

Dave Earley is the director of the Center for Ministry Training at Liberty Theological Seminary (LTS) and chairman of pastoral leadership and church planting at LTS, where he is also a very popular professor. An author and dynamic preacher, Dr. Earley planted and pastored a thriving church in suburban Columbus, Ohio, for twenty years before joining the seminary.

In 1991, just a few years into his church ministry, Pastor Earley was diagnosed with chronic fatigue immune deficiency syndrome. At first he thought it was a bad case of the flu. However, as the recurring pain, loss of energy, pervasive body aches, and inexplicable despair continued, he realized it was more serious.

As he describes his debilitating fatigue, "It was like I was wearing cement and trying to run underwater. I woke up exhausted and stayed exhausted all day long. I used to lie in bed and concentrate on mustering all of my strength so I could turn over by myself. I had been a varsity athlete in college, and yet, at one point I was so weak the only thing I could do all day was crawl down the hall to the bathroom."

His church was in a significant season of growth. With three young sons at home and his lack of energy, his wife bore a disproportionate share of the load. The result was Pastor Earley struggled with horrendous guilt about the little he could accomplish. His burden was intense: "I was frustrated from being the slave of my pain and fatigue. I was frustrated because I was a goal-oriented person who was now unable to pursue any goal other than survival."

There were many days when Earley could not even pray. He was angry at himself and confused with God. He explains,

> The only response I could get from Him was silence—blank, empty, hollow, deafening silence. I constantly asked for deliverance, or at least an explanation, or at the very least a time frame for my agony. Yet, day after day, week after week, month after month, God said nothing. My illness stretched into years. Yet on this issue I received only silence. My soul was dry and my heart broken.
>
> I hate to admit it, but eventually I reasoned that if God would no longer speak to me, then I would not speak to Him, and for a period of weeks I had almost no prayer life.[8]

In time, Earley realized his need to attempt prayer. So, little by little, he began to say thanks and tried to sing praises. He made little progress until the day he experienced a breakthrough. As he describes it, "I received a card from my mom. She had plenty of health problems of her own, yet did not let it stop her. The essence of her card said, 'Quit griping and get going again.'

"As I read it I almost laughed out loud. I had come way too far with God in my life to give up on Him now. So finally I began to tell God I would love Him and serve Him *even if*. *Even if* I never got well. *Even if* He never answered my prayers. *Even if* He never gave me any explanation. And a funny thing happened. I began to get noticeably better."

And so he began to move from being a victim to a place of victory in the midst of his pain.

Getting better has been a very slow process for Dave. It has been well over a decade since he first got sick. He still battles his chronic condition every day. Through it all, he has learned what every leader must learn, "Brokenness and pain must be embraced because they are the tools God loves to use to mold His most effective leaders. God uses wounds to reveal and remove those aspects of our character that are not Christlike."

Christlikeness, then, is yet another fruit of our painful experiences. Dr. Earley discovered it during his fatiguing illness. I discovered it during my brokenness when hurting congregants sought to hurt me. By God's grace, I realized I needed to trade in my self-pity for a pursuit of Jesus Himself. I realized that if I was going to be a Christian leader, I had to identify with Christ.

Yes, I had been wounded. But so had Jesus in ways more excruciating. Separation from God. Mocking. Actual physical torture. He deserved none of His wounds. He took the nails, the thorns, the spear, and the torturous death of the cross for undeserving sinners. As He hung, suspended between heaven and earth, bleeding on the wood of ultimate injustice, He cried, "Father, forgive them, for they do not know what they do" (Luke 23:34).

Unlike Christ, I knew that a fair portion of my wounds were self-inflicted and well-deserved. If the Perfect One could forgive and learn obedience "by the things which He suffered" (Hebrews 5:8), then certainly I could release my detractors from my judgment, bless them, learn the lessons, and move on with a glorious limp. I needed to become more like Jesus and less like myself.

Remember, the time of your pain is a time to draw closer to Christ, to learn of Him, and, finally, to become more like Him.

Open Wounds, Tender Scabs, Empowering Scars

Our open wounds eventually become tender scabs. Fresh from our pain, we can still be a bit fragile and reactive to things that remind us of our previous wounds. But as we endure, the tender scabs become empowering scars. These are scars of authenticity. Through our wounds God "notarizes" our leadership as true and authoritative.

I've always loved Paul's undisputed statement of his credibility as a leader in reply to his critics. Facing the recurring pain of criticism and personal attack, he wrote, "From now on let no one trouble me, for I bear in my body the marks of the Lord Jesus" (Galatians 6:17). The marks of pain are a crucial component of every leadership instrument panel. Remember them. Trust them. They are your friends through the turbulent seasons of life.

Pastor Wells says our pain, whether physical, emotional, or mental, is "much more important than even our formal education." He calls the times of pain part of "the school of woundedness." As such those times are "crucial, because God's grace is going to flow to the humble and broken. Grace is lavished on those who recognize how desperate they are for God. Otherwise, we can become too impressed with our knowledge, gifts, or experience."

Thus pain has surprising benefits, and that's why we need not fear it when we come across the gauge of indispensable pain on the instrument panel of enduring leadership.

Learn to trust your great moments.

CHUCK MILHUFF
Nazarene evangelist

. . . called according to [His] design and purpose.

ROMANS 8:28 (AMP)

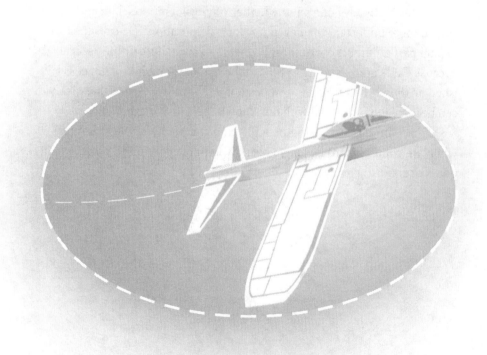

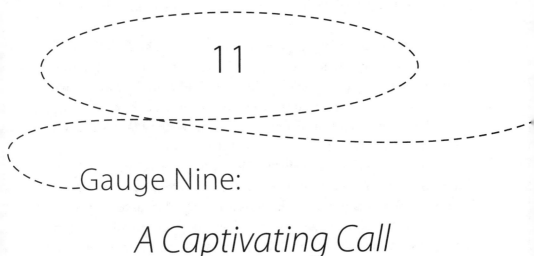

11

Gauge Nine:

A Captivating Call

At age thirty-eight, Sid Verdoorn was named president of C. H. Robinson, a domestic company that specialized in the shipment of fruits and vegetables. Twenty-five years later, when Verdoorn retired, the company had experienced an average growth rate of 19.5 percent per year. Today C. H. Robinson's gross revenues top $7.3 billion with 218 offices worldwide as they provide a diverse array of national and global transportation services.

Verdoorn speaks humbly of his journey, saying, "There is no doubt that God's hand put me in that position." Sid, who is also my friend and mentor, notes God's providence in very specific ways, especially in how he met his wife, Carol, and how her deep spirituality and keen insight about people have been a key to his success.

He saw God's direction throughout his career, beginning with some last-minute changes during the week he was hired in 1963. He was supposed to go to Peoria, Illinois. Instead, he was assigned to a sales desk across the hall from the company president in Minneapolis. Sid spent six years opening the company's San Francisco office in the late sixties, which was another "right place at the right time" scenario. When he was moved back to the corporate headquarters in Minneapolis to assist the company president and serve as director of personnel, he saw God's goodness and direction in it all.

As he describes his later appointment as president, Verdoorn reflects, "Sure I had some skills, but a lot of people had great skills. I was only thirty-eight while other vice presidents and managers were in their forties and fifties. I was raised on a potato farm and did not even have a college education. But circumstance and opportunities aligned in my life in such a way that it was clear to me that it was ultimately God's hand."[1]

That sense of calling kept Sid humble, focused, and accountable in his role as company president. Many times circumstances could have shaken him, but he always came back to the providence of God in his business journey. Even on the day he was named president, one of the branch managers was so upset he sold all of his C. H. Robinson stock. That reaction encouraged Sid to focus again, not on the opinions of people or circumstances, but on God's plan for his life. The reaction also ultimately lost that branch manager about $10 million.

Called by His Name

In many places, God describes His people as those "called by His name" (Deuteronomy 28:10; 2 Chronicles 7:14; Isaiah 43:7; 63:19; Jeremiah 14:9; Daniel 9:19). This connection between a calling and the mighty name of God is the assurance that God's initiative and character are the foundation of our service. When God puts His name on something, it is a done deal and cannot be revoked.

In the New Testament, Christians are described as those who have been called by God into His life and mission through Christ (see "Called by God through Christ"). Again, this invitation comes from God and is maintained by God, in spite of our failures and foibles that often hinder our obedience to the call.

Called by God through Christ

The New Testament describes those in God through Christ as the "called," and we are called into His service and mission in every area of our lives, including the workplace. Here are several of the descriptions of our calling:

- Called of Jesus Christ; called according to His purpose (Romans 1:6–7, 16; 8:28–30; 9:24)
- Called into the fellowship of God's Son, Jesus Christ (1 Corinthians 1:2, 9)
- Called into the grace of Christ (Galatians 1:6)
- A calling that gives hope (Ephesians 1:18; 4:4)
- A calling that gives God's peace (Colossians 3:15)
- Called to God's kingdom and glory (1 Thessalonians 2:12; 5:24; 2 Thessalonians 2:14)
- Called to be holy, "according to His own purpose and grace which was given to us in Christ Jesus" (2 Timothy 1:9; 1 Peter 1:15–16)
- Called to His eternal glory (1 Peter 5:10)

Romans 11:29 affirms this truth, "For the gifts and the calling of God are irrevocable." Eugene Peterson describes it this way in *The Message*, "God's gifts and God's call are under full warranty—never canceled, never rescinded." I am often encouraged by Paul's affirmation of our calling where he says that God has "saved us and called us with a holy calling, not according to our works, but according to His own purpose and grace which was given to us in Christ Jesus before time began" (2 Timothy 1:9). As leaders who have received tasks, we are not just called to "hang in there." Rather we should live in the confidence that God has handed us a calling that is specific to our lives yet greater than ourselves.

Leaders Sustained by a Call

The Scripture presents leaders as having a special and specific call from God. Knowing the call came from God strengthened and sustained three prophets and an apostle as they faced opposition and pain.

The prophet Jeremiah's call came to him as a young man with God's reassurance that before he was even conceived or born, God knew him and set him apart (Jeremiah 1:4–5). In spite of this, the young man initially balked, noting his age and lack of speaking ability. God countered Jeremiah's reluctance with the reassurance that He would be with the prophet to deliver and strengthen him at all times (Jeremiah 1:8, 19). Later, Jeremiah faced persecution and reproach. His heart was again sustained in the truth of God's presence and promise as the prophet confessed, "For I am called by Your name, O Lord God of hosts" (Jeremiah 15:16).

The prophet Ezekiel was warned of the difficulty of his calling as he would speak to a stubborn, hardheaded people. But God gave him this reassurance, "Behold, I have made your face strong against their faces, and your forehead strong against their foreheads. Like adamant stone, harder than flint, I have made your forehead; do not be afraid of them, nor be dismayed" (Ezekiel 3:8–9). With the call came the capability of endurance.

The prophet Isaiah describes the power of a call in Isaiah 49:1–2. It not only reflects the prophet's understanding of a calling, but also refers to the calling of the Messiah, "The Lord has called Me from the womb; from the matrix of My mother He has made mention of My name. And He has made My mouth like a sharp sword; in the shadow of His hand He has hidden Me, and made Me a polished shaft; in His quiver He has hidden Me." I've heard it said that the call of God will not take you where the grace of God cannot keep you. We see this message throughout the Bible.

The assurance of a calling also sustained the apostle Paul. Not only did he refer to it constantly as the power and authority behind all he did (see the first verse of most of the letters he penned), but he boldly explained the sustaining power of this calling in the midst of hardship. In describing his call, Paul reflects on this message from the Lord that carried the clear warning of suffering, "Go, for he is a chosen vessel of Mine to bear My name before

Gentiles, kings, and the children of Israel. For I will show him how many things he must suffer for My name's sake" (Acts 9:15–16).

Paul's very last letter contains an explanation of the sustaining power of the call. Encouraging the endurance of his disciple Timothy, he writes, "I was appointed a preacher, an apostle, and a teacher of the Gentiles. For this reason I also suffer these things; nevertheless I am not ashamed, for I know whom I have believed and am persuaded that He is able to keep what I have committed to Him until that Day" (2 Timothy 1:11–12).

Trust the Call

We've captured this same principle in our day with the simple reminder, "Do not doubt in darkness what God has revealed to you in the light." We must trust the call of God as we encounter the inevitable storms of leadership and service.

One day I sat in a classroom with hundreds of ministry students listening to a Nazarene evangelist named Chuck Milhuff. When asked about the key to knowing God's will, Milhuff offered an answer that was outside the box but has proven to be true and powerful in my life over these years of leadership: "Learn to trust your great moments." He went on to remind these future leaders that God was active in their lives, working through circumstances, instructing through His Word, and guiding through the wisdom of others. He explained that "great moments" of clarity, direction, and calling must be recorded and trusted as key indicators for future decisions and resolve.

Taking Milhuff's advice, I have made it a habit to journal extensively over the years. The several journals I've filled are like the "memorials" of biblical times that always reminded God's people of their great moments like the Passover and crossing the Jordan River. Countless times I have referred back to these journal entries to trust my great moments and receive clear reminders of God's work and calling in my life.

Leading in the Confidence of the Call

Mark DeYmaz was at the "top of his game" as a youth pastor, serving in a very large suburban church in Little Rock, Arkansas. Through a series of observations and some intense biblical study, Mark began to feel a strong calling to plant a different kind of church.

"On May 17, 2001, my wife, Linda, and I responded in prayer to a very specific, yet new seasonal call of God on our lives," he recalls. "That day, we committed ourselves and our family to a journey of faith, courage, and sacrifice that would lead to the establishment of a multiethnic and economically diverse church in the heart of Central Arkansas—a church founded in response to the prayer of Jesus Christ for unity and patterned after the New Testament church at Antioch (Acts 11:19ff.)—a church for others, for all people; a church we called Mosaic."

As of this writing, he continues to serve as directional leader of Mosaic Church of Central Arkansas, operating with a strong sense of God's calling. He affirms that every believer has a *general call* to serve the Lord with his or her life. He also speaks of the *specific call* to full-time vocational service. Finally, Mark describes the *seasonal call* that God places on leaders in the course of their journey. This seasonal call involves particular assignments the Lord gives us in order to fulfill His plan and purpose. The season can be a few years, or it can last an entire career.

Mark's *seasonal call* to plant and lead Mosaic was spurred by his observation of the segregated nature of American churches that seemed to directly contradict biblical teaching on the diversity and unity of the body of Christ. His ongoing studies from Scripture deepened his burden. In addition to these "intellectual considerations," DeYmaz describes several "unprovoked" instances where God intervened through open doors, personal connections, wise advisors, and reassuring affirmations. Speaking of his journey, he notes, "Leaders who have a strong sense of calling are more likely to persevere through those times of testing and trial that inevitably accompany their work. Therefore, the more careful the pursuit of clear calling on the front end, the more certain of it one will be in the midst of its pursuit, that is, in those times when you feel like giving in or giving up, as well. . . . With this in mind, leaders should patiently pursue new ministry endeavors and not proceed for any other reason than God has clearly spoken."[2]

Hans Finzel (see chapter 3) reflects on his *seasonal call* back in the eighties when he was serving as a missionary in Vienna, Austria. During a particular moment of discouragement, Finzel found an article on a bulletin board featuring a David Frost interview with Billy Graham. In the article, Frost inquired, "When are you going to retire?" Finzel distinctly remembers Graham's response, "God called me to preach. Until the day He tells me to stop preaching, I am going to continue." Not only did that thought encourage Finzel to persevere in his service in Vienna but has shaped the practical advice he often offers to leaders, "Be careful not to rescind your call unless God does."

How Call Almost Missed His Calling

Galen Call (his actual name) is the pastor of Venture Christian Church in Los Gatos, California. Recently retired, Call recalls a time when he became burned out in the first church he served as a senior pastor. He had failed to make adjustments in his overcommitted schedule, and he became deeply discouraged. In spite of his wife's reservations and with little understanding of what it meant to be "released" from his current calling, Galen and his wife, Jeannette, left for another church. It turned out to be a miserable experience but a valuable lesson.

It took me about three months to realize that I had made a huge mistake. Just ten months after arriving at the church, I resigned without a place to go. Not a good idea, but my wife and I were so miserable that we concluded it was the only recourse. There we were, hundreds of miles from family support, no income, and potentially homeless! I contacted every resource I could think of to connect with another church; nothing worked. I prayed earnestly, but it was as though the heavens were brass. God had something more for us than an easy way out of that mess—but I was too confused and afraid to see it that way just yet. Wrong thoughts and questions filled my head. Was the first church a fluke? Why were no doors opening for another opportunity? We couldn't "go back" to where we had been and we had no place to go—we felt deserted. How could I explain to a new church what happened? How could they trust my judgment? I don't even trust me! I was angry, at myself . . . and at God. Was He playing a divine joke on us? Why had He abandoned us?[3]

Understandably, at this point he doubted even his call to full-time ministry. Galen describes a phone call he made to a friend who owned a management company. He was hoping to land a job in this business and pursue a total career change away from vocational ministry. Call writes, "He listened patiently as I explained our predicament, then wisely told me that God had not made a mistake in my call to ministry and that I should not consider something else. He exhorted me to wait on God and learn the lessons He had for us in my 'mistake.' That telephone call stands out in my memory as the turning point in my despair. God used him to reassure me of my calling and prevent me from making yet another error of judgment."

Within a month of that phone conversation, a door opened for Galen and Jeannette through a means they could not have predicted or manipulated. The Calls were "joyfully engaged" at the next church for nineteen years for fruitful ministry. Galen writes, "I wish I could say that I had been wise and mature enough at the time to craft and follow a carefully thought out process for confirming my call. I wasn't. I was in 'the fire' of a severe test and did not know how to find my way out. It was God alone who, in great faithfulness, was present with us in the fiery test. And He made 'the way of escape' when He saw we were ready. At the point when I most deeply doubted His calling on my life, He orchestrated our circumstances to affirm it and to assign us to a new place where His blessings were again evident."[4]

When the Gauges Blur

In my own experience and conversations with other leaders, I've identified several factors that tempt us to take our eyes off this important gauge on the leadership instrument panel. When we do look back at the gauge called captivating call, it often looks blurry.

1. Disillusionment

When I was in my early thirties, I was completely disillusioned with my call as a pastor. After three years in the California congregation where I followed the adulterous predecessor, I was exhausted. Battling distrust, solving financial challenges, resolving the multimillion-dollar lawsuit, fielding huge amounts of criticism, and fending off the "concerned group" that wanted to remove us all from leadership had completely overwhelmed me. I was tired and wounded. My wife was hurt and disheartened. Like Galen Call, I was aggressively researching options outside of pastoral ministry. I felt all my hopes and dreams for ministry had been mercilessly crushed.

Fortunately, our elders had the insight and financial resources to send my wife, Rosemary, and me away to a retreat center that specialized in helping troubled ministry couples. Walt and Fran Becker met with us in their Laguna Beach retreat center for ten days—days that changed our lives. We were able to speak openly of our pain and bitterness. We were free to weep as we processed our anger and disappointment. We read many helpful books and walked the beach every day. In the rest, reflection, and objective counsel of those days, God restored my sense of calling.

DeYmaz describes this part of the leadership journey as the "failure to achieve one's desires or determined goals (no matter the reason), or to fulfill your own expectations or the expectations of others. [They] all contribute to doubting one's call in a particular season of ministry."

I had come to that church with such optimism and dreams for the future. Four years later, I left a wounded but better man. The disillusionments of shattered dreams can either bury our sense of calling or serve as an opportunity to clarify it with renewed humility and resolve.

Call describes the challenge of disillusionment, "Leaders can confuse the dreams they have for their ministry with what God's purposes are for it. When the dreams don't happen, a leader can become disappointed and begin to question whether he has heard God's call. That's a wrong response. He should evaluate whether his dream is God's dream. If not, he needs to do the foundational work of listening to God and then pursue God's vision. If he's convinced that his dream is of the Lord, the fact the dream hasn't been fulfilled may be a matter of timing or the dream being realized in another way than he thought. I think of Moses, who correctly thought himself to be the deliverer of God's people but who wrongly judged the time and manner for his work."[5]

2. Discouragement

Call notes, "Leaders can achieve good things for the glory of God, then find themselves emotionally wiped out. They've done God's will, no question about that, but they have expended all in doing it and find themselves living 'on the fumes' of an empty tank."

I define discouragement as "a temporary loss of perspective" and it most often hits when a leader is tired, sick, or overloaded. As Vince Lombardi said, "Fatigue makes cowards out of us all." And quickly the call may seem far less captivating, at times even nonexistent.

3. Spiritual Attack

Beyond the human elements of emotional, mental, and physical limitations and weaknesses, leaders face the supernatural reality of spiritual warfare. Satan is the dealer of doubt, and he delights in shaking leaders from their calling. The Enemy is incessantly lurking in the shadows, waiting for an opportunity to inject doubt into the mind of a leader. He did so with Jesus in the temptation. "If you are the Son of God . . ." was a challenge to Jesus' identity and calling as the Messiah.

Remember, Satan's attacks are subtle and devious, so we need to "test" whether spiritual attack is the source of the doubt. The wise leader will ask questions like: Why do I feel doubt? When I pray, does it recede? What are trusted counselors telling me?

4. Success

Success can make us think we can do it with or without God's call. We begin to feel independent of the God who called us. DeYmaz describes this challenge well. "I have found that with increasing success in ministry comes a decreasing sense of dependency on God for results. In other words, at the start of every new venture in ministry, one exercises a great deal of prayer, faith, and humility . . . but we are human; and consequently, we tend to forget this in the midst of success! While we may take a measure of credit for obedience and faithfulness in our calling, we should not forget that it is God alone who produces fruit, indeed, that it is He alone who is worthy of praise. We will do well to remember this in the midst of success and to make sure that others do, as well."[6]

Keeping Our Eyes on the Call

As leaders who seek to stay in flight, care for our passengers, and land safely when the time comes, we must soar confidently in the power of God's call. As we've seen, this clarity and assurance is core to our perseverance.

When we struggle with confusion, we must remember, rest, and receive. We must remember the "great moments" of God's call, knowing that unless He clearly rescinds it, we should not. We are wise to rest and take time to care for our physical health through diet and exercise. We must receive objective counsel from those who have seen evidence of our call and can remind us of it when we have seemingly forgotten.

Galen Call summarizes our need to fight for clarity, "A good rule: never make a major decision when you're discouraged! Get rest. Read the Word. Listen to God. Journal your thoughts. Be open with your spouse. Do something fun. Call a good friend and talk. Pick up a biography and see that you aren't the first leader to face discouragement or doubt your call."

Part 3
Reaching the Destination

*I had this expectation that my career would
be one in which I didn't crash an airplane.*

CAPTAIN CHESLEY SULLENBERGER
US Airways pilot,
after a skillful crash landing
in New York's Hudson River

*Take heed to yourself and to the doctrine.
Continue in them, for in doing this you will save
both yourself and those who hear you.*

1 TIMOTHY 4:16

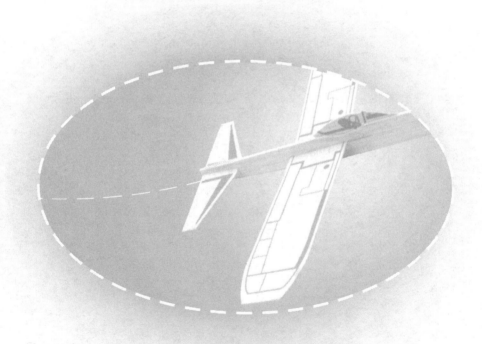

12

Request for an Emergency Landing

Americans will long remember the story of US Airways flight 1549 that crash-landed into New York's Hudson River with all 155 people on board surviving. Captain Chesley Sullenberger became an overnight hero as a result of his incredible skill and coolheaded performance in guiding his disabled aircraft to safety.

In his first public interview after the incident, Sullenberger described the horror of hitting a large flock of birds just ninety seconds after takeoff from LaGuardia Airport. As the engines immediately lost thrust over the densely populated neighborhoods of New York City, the pilot knew he could not return to LaGuardia or reach an alternative runway in time. Later he would tell CBS correspondent Katie Couric, "I knew immediately that this, unlike every other flight I'd had for forty-two years, was probably not going to end with the airplane undamaged on the runway."

In recounting his feelings at the moment, Sullenberger explained, "It was the worst sickening pit of your stomach, falling through the floor feeling I've ever felt in my life. I knew immediately it was very bad." He continued, "My initial reaction was one of disbelief. 'I can't believe this is happening. This doesn't happen to me' . . . I had this expectation that my career would be one in which I didn't crash an airplane."[1]

Like the US Airways captain, leaders sometimes discover that an emergency landing is necessary. It is usually an unintentional and unexpected scenario that requires leaders to act quickly to do everything possible to salvage the plane (the company or ministry) and to save the lives of the passengers.

In moments like this, a leader must accurately assess the prospects of staying in flight and the options for an immediate landing, and then choose a course that will minimize the damage. Captain Sullenberger kept his head clear and his duty intact. In his case, the emergency was required due to mechanical failure. Most leadership emergency landings are connected to human factors that must be understood, responded to, and handled with care and wisdom.

China Airlines 006: Leadership Gone Awry

On February 19, 1985, China Airlines flight 006 requested an emergency landing after a harrowing incident over the Pacific Ocean. This Boeing 747 jetliner was on a routine daily flight from Taipei to Los Angeles when it lost one of its four engines at almost 40,000 feet, ten hours into flight. Even though the experienced three-man cockpit team had several minutes to act, the pilots failed to adjust the controls to counteract the pitch of the plane caused by the failed engine. Through a series of errors and misperceptions, the plane completely rolled over and entered a steep nose-first dive at dangerous speeds through thick clouds.

At one point, the 747 plunged 10,000 feet in just twenty seconds, inflicting the passengers with gravitational forces as high as five g's—pressure five times their body weight.

It was only after breaking through the bottom of the clouds at 11,000 feet that the captain was able to regain his orientation, bring the plane under control, and level out the damaged jetliner at 9,600 feet. In total, the incident had caused the plane to descend 30,000 feet in less than two and a half minutes. Portions of the fuselage and tail had been torn off by the unusual contortions and extreme speed. Two passengers were seriously injured.[2] Rather than landing in Los Angeles, their original destination, they made an emergency landing in San Francisco.

Factors That Lead to an Emergency Landing

The National Transportation and Safety Board (NTSB) conducted extensive investigations of the incident. They concluded that apart from a possible problem with a small valve, nothing was wrong with the plane. This near catastrophe was the result of pilot error. Six factors stand out. Each is relevant to leadership: *fatigue, boredom, distraction, passivity, failure to scan the instruments, and failure to trust the instruments.*[3] It's an intriguing illustration of what can happen in leadership—an unexpected, potentially tragic emergency landing.

In summary, here are the six factors that debilitated the pilots and can affect any leader. During their investigation, the NTSB was baffled that such an experienced crew could make so many mistakes. In their analysis and interviews, they discovered that the first pilot was suffering from severe jet lag at the time of the incident. He had traveled an equivalent of eighteen time zones in the previous six days. The incident occurred at 2:00 a.m. on his natural body clock, a time when his body would normally be in its deepest sleep. Experts concluded that his judgment was impaired by the adverse effects of *fatigue*. This was probably the primary factor that led to a series of mistakes.

One NTSB official also concluded, that the pilot was "bored by the monotony of his tasks." This *boredom* on a long transoceanic flight contributed to inattention and slow response.

Distraction was another factor. Investigators concluded that the crew became overly obsessed with restarting the fourth engine and failed to practice proper procedures for safely piloting the plane. It is "critical that attention be paid to flying the airplane," emphasized aviation expert Delmar Fadden in a National Geographic channel special on the flight. "If the crew becomes so focused on a problem—whether an engine, a lightbulb, or some other malfunction—and no one is flying the plane, disaster results," said Fadden, who also serves as an expert consultant to the NTSB.

Passivity also played a role, the NTSB found. As the autopilot began to turn the plane sharply to the right to compensate for the failed engine, the pilot should have taken control of the plane, using the rudder to keep the 747 on a proper attitude. Instead, he became obsessed with the falling altitude and was trusting the autopilot to make the necessary adjustments.

A significant factor was *the failure of the pilots to scan all the instruments.* The instrument scan is described as a pilot's most basic skill. It involves cross-checking the readings of each instrument with other instruments to confirm an accurate interpretation. The experienced pilot never fixes his view on any single instrument for more than a few seconds, with the occasional exception of the attitude indicator.

In the case of China Airlines 006, investigators believe the chief pilot failed in this very basic discipline. NTSB reports concluded that the pilot was concentrating so rigidly on the airspeed indicator that he failed to notice the attitude indicator instrument right beside it that would have warned him that the plane was, in fact, in a precarious turn. Peter Ladkin, a renowned air disaster consultant, commented on the research: "They (the crew) concentrated on one part of the phenomenon and lost the full picture. As they lost the full picture, they lost, apparently, a very important part of instrument flying, which is the scan. You look at each of the primary instruments one after the other. Whatever is going on, you look at them constantly."[4]

Finally, the investigation indicated that the crew *failed to trust their instruments* as they descended through the clouds without any outside visual reference points. Ladkin again comments, "They simply did not believe what they were seeing. They thought they had lost their attitude instruments." Experts commented by saying that it was hard for the crew to believe what the instruments were telling them, that a 747 had rolled onto its back and was in a vertical dive.

Leaders Heading toward Emergency

China Airlines 006 teaches us some valuable lessons about the factors that cause a "leadership emergency landing" even though we have an instrument panel designed to keep us on course to a safe destination.

1. Fatigue

The China Airlines pilot was jet-lagged. Leaders can easily become "life-lagged"—fatigued with life. Overwork, imbalance, and overall stress can be dangerous, if not monitored. Physical factors can blur a leader's perception, senses, and proper reactions, limiting overall effectiveness. Life-lagged leaders can soon be in an emergency situation, in spite of the reliability of the instruments.

To encourage constant self-monitoring of physical conditions, pilots are taught to regularly review the IMSAFE checklist—a great acrostic to assure the pilot that he or she is safe for flight. Concern about any of the items can become a cause for a pilot to not fly or at least to have a greater awareness of his or her vulnerability to physiological disorientation in flight. The checklist is simple but important:

I *Illness.* Do I have any symptoms?

M *Medication.* Have I been taking any prescription or over-the-counter drugs?

S *Stress.* Am I dealing with any unusual pressures or personal problems?

A *Alcohol.* Have I been drinking in the last eight hours? Twenty-four hours?

F *Fatigue.* Am I tired or inadequately rested?

E *Eating.* Am I adequately nourished for the flight?[5]

Wise leaders create a similar kind of review. Without this, even the best instrument panel cannot guarantee safety in the leadership cockpit. Proper exercise, diet, and rest are essential. Together they allow a leader to properly maximize the instruments and avoid an emergency. Look at the IMSAFE warning list above. Do you have any of these symptoms? If so, the conditions could result in a leadership emergency.

2. Boredom

Although most leadership flights are filled with new initiatives and challenges that keep us invigorated, during the long haul there are times when the routine can cause us to get into a lull.

Settling in to status quo attitudes toward work, marriage, family, and relationships can make a leader vulnerable to surprise and unprepared for crisis.

3. Distraction

As we have already noted, distractions tend to plague many leaders. Taking our eyes off the instrument panel altogether, we can easily find our lives and organizations in a crisis.

Here's another aviation mishap that serves as a reminder of what can go wrong. Almost forty years ago Eastern Air Lines flight crashed into the Florida Everglades, after the crew failed to monitor the flight 401 instruments while working on a faulty landing-gear indicator light. They became so distracted trying to solve the problem with a cheap bulb that they inadvertently flew the plane into the Everglades. Exactly 101 passengers died that cool winter night in December 29, 1972, after the pilots' distraction.

4. Passivity

Passivity can also lead to crisis. In the China Airlines incident, the pilot let the autopilot do what he should have done at a crucial moment. Leaders who are attentive to the instrument panel must act decisively, accurately, and courageously to make the necessary adjustments when indicators signal a problem. If they do not, difficult and risky situations can spiral out of control. Problems ignored become crises unavoided.

5. Failure to Scan the Instruments

Failure to scan the instruments is a subtle and leadership-threatening factor. While each indicator is important, the overall picture of spiritual health gained from constant review of the panel is vital. A complete, ongoing review of the leadership instrument panel will prevent later emergencies in the leader's ministry. Such an overview can be vital to avoiding a leadership emergency. The table "Benefits of a Regular Instrument Review" describes the positive outcomes of reviewing the leadership instrument panel.

- -

Benefits of a Regular Instrument Review

The Leadership Gauge	The Prevention Benefit
1. Applied Truth	False doctrine, superficial teaching, apostasy
2. Spiritual Intimacy	Lack of passion, lack of spiritual power, carnality
3. Personal Integrity	Hypocrisy, compartmentalization, poor example
4. Biblical Identity	Insecurity, drivenness, compromise, overreaction
5. Genuine Accountability	Secret sin, blind spots, isolation
6. Eternal Significance	Discouragement, comparison, loss of reward
7. Healthy Family Life	Surface relationships, pride, moral infidelity
8. Indispensable Pain	Pride, bitterness, resentment
9. A Captivating Call	Giving up, wrong decisions, subjectivity

- -

6. Failure to Trust the Instruments

Throughout this book we've affirmed the essential need to trust the instruments above our own perceptions, self-talk, and emotions. Still, we can be tempted to value our feelings and personal perceptions over the clear readings of the leadership gauges.

Keys to an Honorable Emergency Landing

Regardless of the cause, there are times when an emergency landing is necessary. Maybe, like Captain Sullenberger, something unavoidable has gone wrong with the work situation and the plane is going down. Perhaps, like China Airlines 006, our own errors have led to a daunting moment and we must act to salvage the situation. In any case, let me suggest three key decisions.

1. Gather Objective Input

When your leadership is in crisis, you cannot solve it on your own. Of course, like a pilot, you must return to the gauges. Read them with a keen eye and a cool head. Pray for wisdom in knowing what to do. Ask the Holy Spirit to give you insight.

Invite your flight crew to interpret the indicators with you. When the plane is descending at a rapid pace, that is not the time for subjective conclusions. Selectively invite your spouse, fellow staff, trusted mentors, accountability partners, and others to provide vital input in guiding the plane before an emergency landing is necessary.

Consider a conversation with a trusted spiritual leader, such as your pastor. If you are the pastor, find another trusted pastor. Consider a professional, biblical counselor for objective wisdom.

As I've described earlier in the book, as a young pastor I was in rapid descent after four very painful years of trying to lead a large congregation out of a multifaceted crisis. My elders gave me vital input and eventually funded my wife and me to spend two weeks with a professional couple who specialized in helping clergy couples. I knew I needed to land that leadership plane without forsaking my calling or endangering the passengers, but wanted to do it the right way.

There are times leaders need trusted advisors outside the present situation to assess their wholeness as a leader and to give an objective evaluation of the condition of the plane.

2. Truthful Dialogue with the Tower

In aviation, it is the pilot's responsibility to declare an emergency landing. As China Air 006 regained a steady flight path, the pilots knew they were in trouble. The FAA had lost contact with the plane for a time. Once it was reestablished, the controller asked, "Do you wish to declare an emergency?" At first the pilot was hesitant. However, the facts required it. The landing gear was locked in a down position due to damage sustained in the rapid descent. Two passengers were seriously injured. Pieces of the tail were missing.

Sometimes a leader's pride prevents him or her from being open to the need for an emergency landing. We view it as an admission of failure, which may or may not be the case. Sometimes the factors are beyond our control. Other times, God has lessons from our failures that will make us better leaders in the future. We do learn more from our failures than our successes.

When pride is mingled with pain, the admission is even harder. It becomes personal as we resist the idea of allowing a critic or antagonist to "win." Of course, we have to get beyond the petty and subjective emotions to embrace the greater good in the situation.

3. The Overarching Concerns

This leads us to the overarching concerns in an emergency landing: the honor of Christ, the well-being of the passengers, and the hopeful preservation of the plane (the ministry or company).

By all means, we must salvage the flight in such a way that the approach has honored Christ and His truth—in the dealings of our own heart, in all relationships, in our methods, and in the testimony of His name in the community.

During my early thirties, I knew I was in trouble the very first year of my pastoral assignment. In the midst of trying to regain momentum and rebuild the credibility of the pastoral office, we hit some major turbulence. Through accounting errors by the business office, our auditor discovered that the church had spent $400,000 in designated funds to support the general fund expenses. Of course, we had to immediately address the staff member responsible for the faux pas but then had to lay off additional staff in order to replenish the designated accounts. This picked a very tender scab among many of the already-hurting people in the church. I knew from that moment in the first twelve months that my tenure would be short-term.

Every year during my four years there Pastor Chuck Swindoll visited the church with his ministry interns as part of an annual ministry exposure trip. Pulling my wife and me under his wise leadership wing, he invited us out for coffee each time they visited. His advice was to "move on" as it usually took a decade for churches in this kind of situation to recover. He felt we should find a healthier setting.

Yet, I knew I could not just "bail." So I decided to try and find the closest landing strip. Yet, my staff and elders were insistent that I hang on. All my wise counselors encouraged endurance.

At the same time, the Lord challenged me with this passage, "The good shepherd gives His life for the sheep. But a hireling, he who is not the shepherd . . . sees the wolf coming and leaves the sheep and flees; and the wolf catches the sheep and scatters them. The hireling flees because he is a hireling and does not care about the sheep" (John 10:11–13). I knew God was seeking to make me a Christlike leader and I could not behave like a hireling. I would have to sacrifice much to keep the sheep from scattering and to see the church stay intact.

In time, it was clear that the right airport was on the horizon. Wise counsel helped me see this. My instrument panel kept me together until I could land the plane. The flight only lasted four years. The landing was smooth. I moved on and so did the church.

Numerous times I have been back to preach there. Words cannot describe the deep emotion of looking into the faces of those whom God had entrusted to my care, knowing that we were able to get safely through the storms and they were able to press on in their love for and faith in Christ.

The Ultimate Task: Save Lives

US Airways Captain "Sully" Sullenberger became a hero that day on the Hudson River because he found a way to land a doomed flight in order to save every life on board. This is the ultimate leadership task.

In reflecting on the troubled flight of China Airlines 006, expert Peter Ladkin offered this final commentary, "The one big thing they did right —they saved the airplane. In principle that's all you ever need to do right— you need to save the airplane and save the passengers."

The primary performance that counts is the last one.

A. PIERRE GUILLERMAN
Founding President, Liberty University

*I have fought the good fight, I have finished the race,
I have kept the faith. Finally, there is laid up for me the
crown of righteousness, which the Lord, the righteous
Judge, will give to me on that Day, and not to me only
but also to all who have loved His appearing.*

2 TIMOTHY 4:7–8

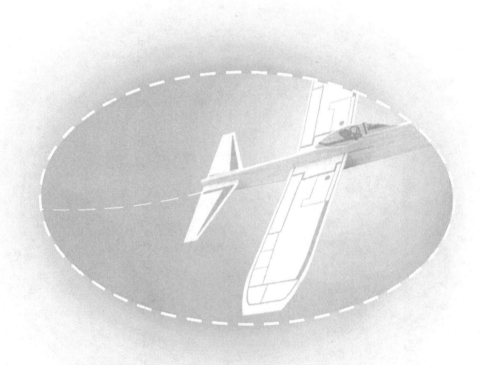

13

The Final Approach

Early during my senior year of college, I sat in a classroom filled with student leaders. It was my second year as student body president, and we had gathered to receive training from our college president, a wise, unassuming man who had a passion for the next generation of change agents.

He said many things that day, but one statement captured my imagination and has stayed with me as a plumb line of vital perspective since then. He declared, "The primary performance that counts is the last one."

We were all just "student pilots" in our leadership flight when he spoke and probably gave little thought at that moment as to how we would eventually land the plane. Filled with youthful ambition and surging with adrenaline, we were charting the course for a year of impact on our campus. However, the wisdom of this insight rang powerfully in my heart. It really does not matter how well you start the leadership journey if you do not finish with honor.

A Solid Landing for a Strong Legacy

While a leader's journey may be composed of numerous leadership flights, the wise leader gives serious consideration to what we are calling the final approach—the final chapter of life and leadership. Real leaders never stop leading. In some form or fashion, with or without a title or office and long after any formal "retirement," they keep influencing lives. Often the integrity and impact of their lives find their finest moment on the final approach.

Stuart Matthews, founder and chief executive officer of the Flight Safety Foundation, notes that "fifty percent of all accidents happen during just four percent of flight time—during approach and landing."[1] In aviation, pilot error, inclement weather, optical illusions, equipment failure, and other factors combine to make this part of the flight so risky. In leadership, it is easy to fall into an unguarded and unfocused mode of "coasting" to the finish. Wisdom compels us to lead well and intently until the very end of the journey.

Many leaders with various exploits to their credit are remembered in infamy due to a catastrophic failure at some juncture. In chapter 12 we considered the necessary "emergency landing," which is still a landing of honor. What we are considering in this final chapter is a disaster brought on by reckless piloting and massive disregard for the leadership instrument panel. You may have defied gravity throughout your leadership flight, yet, now, as you prepare to land, you falter big-time. Whether at the beginning, middle, or end, a crash is still a crash.

I've also known some leaders who faithfully serve an organization but become soured toward the end of their tenure due to a turn of events— maybe a layoff or change of direction in the company. Their previous years of service are negated by a sour-grapes departure and a negative mind-set that lingers.

When I think of how some endgame failure mars the legacy of a leader, I imagine standing on some vista in the mountains looking over beautiful valleys, streams, and rolling ranges. The scene is breathtaking and inspiring. Then I consider what it would be like to raise my fist, holding it an inch from my face. The beautiful view would be blocked by a blurry image of knuckles, skin, hair, and a freckle or two. This illustrates what happens when a leader fails to finish with honor. The image of a powerful and Christ-honoring lifetime of service is eclipsed by an unfortunate and undeniable obstruction.

Unsettling Images

Or consider these unsettling images: a beautiful painting with a black inkblot, a fine car with a completely cracked windshield, a beautiful dinner with a pile of hair on top of the potatoes au gratin, or a freshly roasted cup of Pikes Market blend from Starbucks with a boiled bug floating atop the brew. These pictures all capture the disappointment of a leader who fails to finish honorably.

The Southern Baptist Convention once reported that only one-third of their seminary graduates remain in ministry five years after graduation. So not long ago, I sat at a lunch table with the then-president of the Southern Baptist Convention and asked about the validity of the statistic. He replied, "Yes, it is true, and not only that—another one-third of seminary graduates do not finish honorably in vocational ministry."

John Bisagno is retired pastor of the 22,000–member First Baptist Church of Houston. He began his ministry there in 1970 and was powerfully used of God during his decades of outstanding leadership. Bisagno recounts the story of a conversation he had as a young man with his future father-in-law who spoke of the dangers of leadership and the large numbers of leaders who did not finish well. At the time it seemed almost unbelievable to Bisagno that so many men would start well but not finish honorably.

He tells of how he went home that evening, turned to a blank page in the back of his Bible and wrote down the names of twenty-four of his peers—young men who loved Christ and were sold out to serve Him. These were friends he was confident would stay the course.

Years later, he recounted, "From time to time as the years have gone by, I've had to turn back to that page in my Bible and cross out a name. I wrote down those twenty-four names when I was just twenty years of age. Thirty-three years later, there are only three names remaining of the original twenty-four."[2]

In the business arena, we are all aware of leaders who succeeded in their financial pursuits but crashed and burned in their personal lives, whether through multiple marriages or personal behavior patterns that flushed all their respect down the toilet. Jesus' words ring true, "For what profit is it to a man if he gains the whole world, and loses his own soul?" (Matthew 16:26). We might add, "What does it profit a man to win the short-term financial game but lose the long-term life game?"

The Finishing Kick

In spite of the heartbreaking stories and distressing statistics, the vast majority of leaders do finish well. In this we truly celebrate. As we conclude our consideration of the leadership flight, let's reaffirm the factors that make for a safe, reputable landing—and an honorable, lasting legacy.

Admittedly, the Bible never describes the Christian leadership as a "flight" or piloting exercise. Of course, man-made flight did not exist in biblical days. The closest comparison is the illustration of an eagle. The eagle's flight is a symbol of spiritual vigor (Psalm 103:5; Isaiah 40:31). The eagle is presented as symbolic of God's strength and loving care (Exodus 19:4; Deuteronomy 32:11) and is described as very swift (Job 9:26; Proverbs 23:5). His high nest is also used as a picture of security (Jeremiah 49:16; Obadiah 4).

Scripture does frequently use the metaphor of running a race, so let's depart from the flight imagery and go to the running course as we consider what it means to finish strong and to make an honorable final approach. The Bible describes the Christian life as a race that is definitely more like a marathon than a sprint. The writer of Hebrews calls us to "run with endurance the race that is set before us" (Hebrews 12:1). Paul compels us to run with discipline and resolve to win an eternal prize, cautioning us about the possibility of becoming disqualified (1 Corinthians 9:24–27). He expressed his concern that he would run the race in "vain" (Philippians 2:16; Galatians 2:2). He expressed regret that the believers in Galatia had once run well but had been hindered in their faith (Galatians 5:7).

Every race is judged not by how it starts but how it is finished. The sprinter in the relay race who charges out in the first leg may give his team the lead. But no matter how fast he comes off the starting block to make a handoff to the next runner, it matters for nothing—unless the athlete running the final leg is fast enough to finish the race ahead of the competing teams. The finish matters as much as the beginning.

I've always been impressed with distance runners who know how to excel in a race of multiple laps or even many miles. A key to their perform-ance in long-distance contests is the ability to "kick" in the final segment of the race. Usually the winner's best effort is his last one as he reserves a sprint-like reserve to finish the race at a profound pace.

Choosing How to Finish

Knowing the Christian life is a long-distance event compels each of us to ask the question: How will I finish the race? What will my spiritual pace look like as I approach the finish line? Will my last lap be my best one? Or will I dribble across the finish line with a "spiritual retirement" mind-set, running without purpose?

Paul finished impressively. In what amounted to the final press of his pen to the parchment, he wrote,

> For I am already being poured out as a drink offering, and the time of my departure is at hand. I have fought the good fight, I have finished the race, I have kept the faith. Finally, there is laid up for me the crown of righteousness, which the Lord, the righteous Judge, will give to me on that Day, and not to me only but also to all who have loved His appearing. (2 Timothy 4:6–8)

Paul was so spiritually resolute in his final steps before touching eter-nity's tape that he described his death as an act of worship. He spoke with passion about the grace of God that enabled him to finish his race and spoke with great anticipation of the crown that made every effort worth it.

I'll never forget a time some years ago when I encountered two seventy-two-year-old pastors who were complete opposites in their approach to the last strides in their ministry race. One was retired, grumpy, negative, and aimless. The other was still in the pulpit, gracious, optimistic, and dream-ing about his future. One complained about the younger generation and how they had forsaken the "good old ways" of his ministry preferences. The second was busy investing in young men, with a desire to help them live like Christ. One was stumbling toward the finish line with his head down in despair and morbid introspection. The other had his eyes on the prize with growing spiritual impact as the years went by. It was not hard to decide which model I hope to follow as my golden years approach.

The Ninety-Eight-Year-Old Finisher

Recently I was deeply impressed with a man who attended a three-day Men's Prayer Summit that I led in Minnesota. Chet is ninety-eight years old. Not only was I astonished that he was willing to commit to this very intense, unscripted, multiday prayer experience but even more amazed with his active participation during the entire event. He watched, he listened, he sang, and he prayed with an open heart and joyful attitude.

On the final evening of the summit, we enjoyed a two-hour Communion experience. The service included the option for men to wash the feet of other men at a prayer station in the back of the room, if they felt led to do so. Of course, a handful of younger men were eager to honor Chet by washing his feet. One of our leaders who was observing it all told me that Chet also served some of the other men in this way. He said the entire time Chet was washing their feet he quoted an unbroken array of Scripture passages from memory.

I want to be like Chet when I grow up! That is the attitude and impact I want when I make my final approach—and cross the finish line. What passion, humility, and depth. He is a living picture of Psalm 92:13–15:

Those who are planted in the house of the Lord shall flourish in the courts of our God. They shall still bear fruit in old age; they shall be fresh and flourishing, to declare that the Lord is upright; He is my rock, and there is no unrighteousness in Him.

Secrets to the Finish Line Kick

To understand people like Chet, we do well to turn to the Scriptures to observe some of the keys to running strong to the end. We could say that these are the vital principles for the finishing kick—or returning to our aviation metaphor, vital for the final approach. Paul's personal commentary from Acts 20:24 gives us great insight. He was on his way to Jerusalem knowing he would suffer there for the cause of Christ yet unsure what would actually happen (v. 22). Still, he made this bold declaration: "But none of these things move me; nor do I count my life dear to myself, so that I may finish my race with joy, and the ministry which I received from the Lord Jesus, to testify to the gospel of the grace of God." Here we see Paul's determination to finish his race. Looking at the apostle's words, let's observe five key insights for a strong final lap:

1. *Seeing beyond the moment.* Even though "chains and tribulations" awaited Paul, he wrote "none of these things move me" (vv. 23–24). Paul saw beyond the present press and pain of circumstances to the good and Christ-honoring eventual outcome. We've already noted this kind of eternal perspective and spiritual vision that empowers us to grasp the real meaning of life. I remember an interview I conducted with pastor and university chancellor Jerry Falwell, who told me that "real vision never allows you the luxury of discouragement."

2. *Letting go and living.* Paul also told his readers, "Nor do I count my life dear to myself" (v. 24). Jesus made it clear that when we try and preserve our life, we lose it (Matthew 16:25). Sacrifice for the cause of Christ is a life-giving reality for the believer. The gray twilight of halfhearted commitment is the dead zone that robs leaders of passion and impact.

3. *Having joy like Jesus.* Paul was determined to finish his race with joy. This is just like Jesus, the author and finisher of our faith, "who for the joy that was set before Him endured the cross, despising the shame, and has sat down at the right hand of the throne of God" (Hebrews 12:2). Joy comes, not from easy circumstances or an absence of suffering in the final chapters of leadership, but from knowing it is always worth it in light of the eternal reward.

4. *Being a steward who serves.* Paul remained motivated by "the ministry which (he) received from the Lord Jesus." Later in this same

sermon, Paul quoted Jesus stating that it is more blessed (or happy) to give than to receive (Acts 20:35). Givers are always happier and healthier. They see themselves as stewards responsible to bless others with all they have been given—especially as they have the finish line in sight. Hoarders are miserable and weary. They finish their race laboring under a load of self-absorbed care.

5. *Keeping the mission central.* Paul lived to "testify to the gospel of the grace of God." His life was not about himself but focused on the greatest cause in the world. This kind of purpose ennobles and invigorates a life that ends well. As I think of Chet's passionate prayers for three days and his deep devotion to the Scriptures, I know that he is a man fully devoted to the mission of Jesus in this world. Although long since retired from his successful business career, he has remained loyal to his greater calling to know Christ and make Him known.

Some leaders live their final years with hardening of the arteries. Others finish with hardening of the attitudes, which is much worse. We must pray that God will keep our attitudes soft and hearts passionate so that our final effort will be our best as we cross the finish line of this race into the reward to eternal glory in the presence of Jesus—the Joyful Finisher!

Mission Accomplished

I fly a lot these days, speaking in churches and leadership conferences. Frankly, I do not think a lot about the dynamics of these flights. Usually I am preoccupied with some reading I need to do, working on my laptop computer, or talking to a fellow passenger. Of course, takeoff usually provides the perfect moment for a power nap. Less experienced travelers tend to tune in to every part of the flight instructions, react to every hint of turbulence, and sigh with relief when the plane lands.

Still, there is one part of every flight that is truly my favorite. It occurs as passengers file off the plane. The captain stands by the cockpit door, looks every passenger in the eye, and says something like, "Thanks for flying with us today."

That has to be a pretty cool feeling. I imagine it is the fulfillment of a mission accomplished. The passengers have arrived safely. They are off to their next business meeting, a family reunion, or a welcomed night in their own bed. But the captain knows that he has done his job with excellence and honor. He completed the flight plan and landed the plane. He or she has been a faithful steward of the trust of the passengers and flown with honor for the company the captain represents.

This is part of the expectation of a leader who defies gravity and soars in his leadership service. This is the joy of a leader who kept altitude, trusted the instruments, and made the final approach with honor. This is the fulfillment of the leadership journey, knowing that souls entrusted to our care have made their needful destination. Yes, the primary performance that counts is the last one.

Perhaps the greatest reward is the hope of stepping out of the cockpit and onto the Jetway to eternity. There, awaiting every faithful leader is the "captain of [our] salvation" (Hebrews 2:10) who will look into our eyes and announce, "Well done, good and faithful servant; you have been faithful over a few things, I will make you ruler over many things. Enter into the joy of your Lord" (Matthew 25:23).

Notes

Introduction

1. James C. Dobson, "The Titanic. The Church. What They Have in Common," Focus on the Family Monthly Newsletter, August 1998; at http://www2.focusonthefamily.com/docstudy/newsletters/A000000803.cfm. The figure is based on a compilation of surveys from Focus on the Family pastors gatherings. In addition, 80 percent of pastors surveyed said they are discouraged or dealing with depression.

2. George Barna, *The Second Coming of the Church* (Nashville: Word, 1998), 5.

Chapter 1: Unexpected Leadership Storms

1. "The Spirit of St. Louis Story," http://www.charleslindbergh.com/hall/spirit.asp.

2. Charles Lindbergh, *The Spirit of St. Louis* (New York: Scribner & Sons, 1953); as cited in Lamar Underwood, *The Greatest Flying Stories Ever Told* (Guilford, Conn.: Lyons Press, 2002), 5.

Chapter 2: Trusting the Leadership Instruments

1. Joan Walsh, Daryl Lindsey, and Anthony York, "Graveyard Spiral: Did Bad Judgment or Bad Luck Doom JFK Jr.?"; at www.salon.com/news/feature/1999/07/20/reckless/index.html.

2. "Fatal Aircraft Crash Involving John F. Kennedy, Jr."; http://www.airsafe.com/events/celebs/jfk_jr.htm; and www.ntsb.gov/ntsb/brief.asp?ev_id=20001212X19354&key=1.

3. *Instrument Flying Handbook, U.S. Department of Transportation* (Oklahoma City: Federal Aviation Administration, 2007), 1–1.

4. *Guided Flight Discovery: Instrument Commercial* (Englewood, Colo.: Jeppesen Sanderson, 2003), 1–3.

5. Samuel D. Rima, *Leading from the Inside Out: The Art of Self-Leadership* (Baker: Grand Rapids, 2000), 194.

6. *Guided Flight Discovery*, 1–8.

7. Ibid., 1–12.

Chapter 3: Gauge One: Applied Truth

1. John MacArthur, personal telephone interview, 14 January 2009.

2. Ibid.

3. Paul Powers, e-mail interview, 29 November 2008.

4. Hans Finzel, telephone interview, 19 December 2008.

5. Ibid.

6. Ibid.

Chapter 4: Gauge Two: Spiritual Intimacy

1. See these examples: Abraham (Genesis 21:22), Isaac (Genesis 21:20; 26:3, 24, 28), Jacob (Genesis 28:15, 20; 31:3, 42), Joseph (Genesis 39:2, 21, 23; 48:21), Moses (Exodus 3:12; 33:15–16; Joshua 1:17), Joshua (Joshua 1:5, 17; 3:7; 6:27; 7:12), Gideon (Judges 6:12, 16), Samson (Judges 13:24; 14:6, 19; 15:14; 16:20), Samuel (1 Samuel 2:21; 3:19). Among the kings of Israel, read about Saul (1 Samuel 10:7), David (1 Samuel 16:13; 17:37; 18:12, 14, 28; 20:13; 2 Samuel 5:10; 7:3; 1 Kings 1:37; 1 Chronicles 11:9; 17:8), Solomon (1 Kings 1:37; 8:57; 1 Chronicles 22:18; 28:20; 2 Chronicles 1:1), Asa (2 Chronicles 15:2, 9), Jehoshaphat (2 Chronicles 17:3; 19:11; 20:17), Uzziah (2 Chronicles 26:5), and Hezekiah (2 Kings 18:7; 2 Chronicles 31:21; 32:8). Two other notable Old Testament leaders were Ezra (Ezra 1:3; 8:18, 22, 31) and Nehemiah (Nehemiah 2:8, 18; 4:20); and one great New Testament leader empowered by God's Spirit was John the Baptist (Luke 1:66).

2. See Acts 1:13–14, 24; 2:42; 3:1; 4:24–31; 6:4; 9:40; 10:9; 12:5, 12; 13:1–3.

3. Jim Shaddix, e-mail interview, 1 December 2008.

4. Ibid.

5. E. M. Bounds, *The Weapon of Prayer*, in *The Complete Works of E. M. Bounds* (Grand Rapids: Baker, 1990), 370–71.

6. Peter Lord and Daniel Henderson, *The 29:59 Plan* (Forest, Virg.: Strategic Renewal); www.pray2959.com.

7. I have written extensively about how this works in our lives and ministries in Daniel Henderson, *Fresh Encounters: Experiencing Transformation through United Worship-based Prayer* (Colorado Springs: NavPress, 2004).

8. Gene Getz, *Praying for One Another* (Wheaton, Ill.: Victor, 1982), 11–12.

9. David Peddie, telephone interview, 12 December 2008.

Chapter 5: Gauge Three: Personal Integrity

1. Merriam-Webster's Online Medical Dictionary, http://www.merriam-webster.com/medical/compartmentalization.

2. *Dexter*, Showtime-TV, season 2, episode 12:00:46:04-00:46:10.

3. http://www.merriam-webster.com/dictionary/integrity.

4. See *Keil & Delitzsch Commentary on the Old Testament*, vol. 5 (Grand Rapids: Eerdmans, 1980), 211; also Eugene H. Merrill, *Kingdom of Priests: A History of Old Testament Israel* (Grand Rapids: Baker, 1987), 244–45.

Chapter 6: Gauge Four: Biblical Identity

1. Daniel Henderson, *The Seven Most Important Questions You'll Ever Answer* (Forest, Virg.: Strategic Renewal, 1998), 62.

2. *Wall Street Journal*, no date, by United Technologies Corporation, Hartford, Connecticut, as quoted in Warren Bennis and Burt Nanus, *Leaders: Strategies for Taking Charge* (New York: Harper and Row, 1985), 22.

3. Abraham Maslow, *Toward a Psychology of Being* (New York: Van Nostrand Reinhold, 1968).

4. Paul Hontz, telephone interview, 2 December 2008.

5. See, for example, the chart "Who I Am in Christ," in Neil Anderson, *Living Free in Christ* (Ventura, Calif.: Regal, 1993).

6. I describe the daily renewal system in Henderson, *The Seven Most Important Questions*. Readers are guided to find biblical answers to the seven questions: Who is God? Who am I? Why am I here? What really matters? What should I do? When should I do it? How should I do it? This approach creates a daily renewal process of thinking biblically about the seven issues of theology, identity, purpose, values, priorities, goals, and time.

7. Dave Gudgel, e-mail interview, 8 November 2008.

Chapter 7: Gauge Five: Genuine Accountability

1. Ken Blanchard, *The Servant Leader* (Nashville: Thomas Nelson, 2003), 104–5.

2. John MacArthur, telephone interview, 14 January 2009.

3. Luis Bush, e-mail interview, 22 November 2008.

4. As used by Paul Molitor with a group of men who met with Pastor Dave Gibson at Grace Church, Eden Prairie, Minnesota.

5. Paul Molitor, telephone interview, 16 December 2008.

6. Sid Verdoon, telephone interview, 2 December 2008.

7. MacArthur, interview.

8. A very practical and powerful tool for personal renewal and prevention is available for download at www.strategicrenewal.com/40reasons. The piece, entitled "Forty Reasons Why I Do Not Want to Commit Adultery," has proven to be a helpful tool to thousands of pastors in avoiding the consequences of moral failure. It reminds leaders of their own vulnerability and the need to always take the positive path of purity.

9. Paul Powers, part of e-mail interview, 29 November 2008.

Chapter 8: Gauge Six: Eternal Significance

1. Vernon Brewer, e-mail interview, 17 December 2008.

2. Karen Covell, e-mail interview, 1 December 2008.

3. Ibid.

4. Ibid.

5. Vernon Brewer, e-mail correspondence, 17 December 2008.

6. As quoted in Simpson's *Contemporary Quotations*, comp., James B. Simpson (New York: Houghton Mifflin, 1988), number 4183.

Chapter 9: Gauge Seven: Healthy Family Life

1. Dennis Henderson, e-mail interview, 22 January 2009. Dennis is my older brother.

2. For more information, see www.mondaymorningministry.com.

3. Henderson, e-mail interview.

4. Wynn Kenyon, "Family Traits," *Tabletalk*, Ligonier Ministries, March 2007, 14.

5. Ken Nair, *Discovering the Mind of a Woman* (Nashville: Nelson, 1995), 52–53. I've used this book over the years to train young male leaders in developing a proper attitude toward marriage and family, and I highly recommend it.

6. Doug Boquist, e-mail interview, 1 December 2008.

Chapter 10: Gauge Eight: Indispensable Pain

1. Jennifer Dean, personal interview, 4 December 2008.

2. C. S. Lewis, *The Problem of Pain* (New York: Macmillan, 1996), 91.

3. Oswald Chambers, *My Utmost for His Highest* (Grand Rapids: Discovery House, 1992), September 30.

4. Charles Spurgeon, *Spurgeon's Sermons on Great Prayers of the Bible* (Grand Rapids: Kregel, 1995), 31.

5. Jeff Wells, personal interview, 3 December 2008.

6. A. W. Tozer, *The Dwelling Place of God* (Harrisburg, Pa.: Christian Publications, 1966), 85.

7. Rick Warren, *The Purpose Driven Life* (Grand Rapids: Zondervan, 2002), 297.

8. David Earley, e-mail interview, 9 December 2008.

Chapter 11: Gauge Nine: A Captivating Call

1. Sid Verdoorn, telephone interview, 2 December 2008.

2. Mark DeYmaz, e-mail interview, 28 November 2008.

3. Galen Call, e-mail interview, 24 November.

4. Ibid.

5. Ibid.

6. DeYmaz interview.

Chapter 12: Request for an Emergency Landing

1. Interview with Katie Couric, *60 Minutes*, CBS-TV, 5 February 2009.

2. Peter Ladkin, *Panic over the Pacific*, National Geographic television, January 2009.

3. Ibid.

4. Ibid.

5. *Instrument Flying Handbook, US Department of Transportation* (Oklahoma City: Federal Aviaton Administration, 2007), 1–13.

Chapter 13: The Final Approach

1. Stuart Matthews, *Flight Safety Foundation News* (Alexandria, Virg.: Flight Safety Foundation), 18 December 1996.

2. As cited in Steve Farrar, *Finishing Strong* (Sisters, Oreg.: Multnomah, 1995), 6.

The Wound

They didn't warn me about the wound in seminary
So it has come as quite a shock to my unsuspecting heart.

At times it seems so deep—beyond the repair of stitches.
Even divine sutures seem insufficient and vain;
The breadth of the wound overwhelms me at moments:
All consuming—defeating—debilitating.

Then, some days the wound is inconsequential.
I busy myself with administrivia to anesthetize its presence.
I try to enjoy my family and hope it doesn't surface.
After the well-delivered Sunday sermon, I forget it is there.

But by Monday, its stench and pain has reappeared,
Creating a noticeable limp in my ministerial gait
And a dullness to my vision and faith.

I would like to ignore it: just pretend it's not true.
But its dull, sometimes sharp prompting won't leave me alone.
It goes with me—following me everywhere—
Within me at all times, reminding me constantly.

It has become the unwelcome mirror of my weakness and vulnerability.

The wound is a grinding present memory of my failures;
Its reality shoots through the nervous system of my inner-man,
Calling out for attention, at least a fair estimation.

So now, in these quiet moments, I sit—
face to face with my woundedness.
Oh, my wound—my horrible wound—you unwelcomed intruder
Why have you come? Why won't you go?

Perhaps I have no recourse but to make you my friend.
You must know that I would not have chosen you as a companion,
For in so many ways you are ugly and troublesome to me.
But now, I must love you, embrace you—
integrate you gladly into the very fabric of my being.

What? What is that you say?
You are the intimate friend of my Savior Jesus?
You found your discriminating way into His life?
His hands, His feet, His brow, His side are marked by your presence?
His heart, too, wears your brand?

Oh wound—precious wound. Forgive me, for I did not understand.
It is you that gave my Master the privilege of suffering for me.
By you I was forgiven and healed, in Him.

So I must welcome you, beloved wound.
Yes, make yourself a part of me.
Offer your touch to the hurting world around me,
that they too may see your wonder—
and know your healing grace.

Oh wound, you are my enigma.
But you are my friend.
Without warning you came.
Now, without question—please, please—stay.

© 1999, 2010 by Daniel Henderson

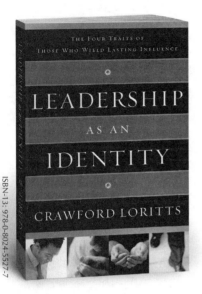

SPIRITUAL LEADERSHIP

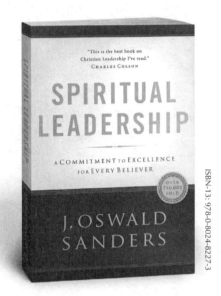

The biblical call to leadership must not be taken lightly. And with more than 750,000 sold, *Spiritual Leadership* has proven itself a timeless classic in teaching the key principles of leadership. J. Oswald Sanders presents and illustrates several magnifying principles through the lives of some prolific men—men such as Moses, Nehemiah, Paul, David Livingstone, and Charles Spurgeon. *Spiritual Leadership* will encourage you to place your talents and powers at God's disposal so you can become a leader used for his glory. An updated, modern flavor and a growth-empowering study guide allow *Spiritual Leadership* to forge ahead, forming the next generation of leaders.

MOODY
PUBLISHERS

1-800-678-8812 • MOODYPUBLISHERS.COM